TWAYNE'S WORLD AUTHORS SERIES

A Survey of the World's Literature

YUGOSLAVIA

John Loud, Texas Christian University

EDITOR

Francè Prešeren

TWAS 620

Francè Prešeren (1800-1849)

FRANCÈ PREŠEREN

By HENRY RONALD COOPER, JR.
Northwestern University

TWAYNE PUBLISHERS
A DIVISION OF G. K. HALL & CO., BOSTON

Library of Congress Cataloging in Publication Data

Cooper, Henry R
France Prešeren.

(Twayne's world authors series ; TWAS 620 : Yugoslavia)
Bibliography: p. 158-61
Includes index.
1. Prešeren, France, 1800-1849.
2.   Authors, Slovenian—19th century—Biography.
PG1918.P7Z6   891.8′414   80-29612
ISBN 0-8057-6462-3

pd
1-26-85

To Professor Rado L. Lencek

VIOLA: "What country, friends, is this?"
CAPTAIN: "This is Illyria, lady."
VIOLA: "And what should I do in Illyria?"
Shakespeare, *Twelfth Night*

Contents

About the Author

Preface

Chronology

Map of Slovenia

About the Author

A teacher of Russian, Polish, and Czech as well as Slovene, Henry R. Cooper, Jr. has been an assistant professor of Slavic languages at Northwestern University for the past six years. He holds a doctoral degree in Slavic literatures from Columbia University, and has studied in France, Germany, the Soviet Union, Yugoslavia, and Bulgaria. His scholarly interests include Old Russian literature (he is the author of *The Igor Tale: An Annotated Bibliography of 20th Century Non-Soviet Scholarship on the Slovo o polku Igoreve* [White Plains and London, 1978]), Polish literature, Slavic civilizations, comparative literature (his dissertation examined late Italian Renaissance literary influences in Slavic literatures), and most recently Slovene literature, language, and culture. He is the editor of the journal *Slovene Studies*, a member of the executive council of the Society for Slovene Studies, the organizer of "The Conference to Honor Jernej Kopitar, 1780-1980" (a symposium to examine the contributions of the founder of Slovene and Balkan studies), and the editor of, and a contributor to, *Papers in Slovene Studies, 1978*. In addition he has served on the editorial boards of *Canadian-American Slavic Studies* and *Balkanistica*, and reviews books for *The Slavic and East European Journal*. Cooper's current projects include an introduction to Russian poetry for college freshmen, a Polish teaching grammar for Slavists, an article on humanism in medieval Muscovy, as well as a paper on Oton Župančič, the greatest Slovene poet of the twentieth century.

Preface

This book, the first of its kind in English, is an apology for Francè Prešeren, the greatest of Slovenia's poets. As such it makes one fundamental assumption, that most who read it know nothing or almost nothing about either the man or his poetry, and very little about his country. My goal from the outset has been, therefore, to shed light on Prešeren, so that the reader of this volume might gain some insight into his life, poetic practice, themes, and position in the literary history of his homeland. To accomplish this task, I have sought to act for the English reader as an interpreter of the mass of scholarship—over 6,500 items are recorded in the *Prešeren Bibliography*—which has been written about the poet in Slovene, Serbo-Croatian, German, Italian, and other languages. If I convince my reader that the obscurity surrounding this genial poet of a small nation is unjustified, then I will judge my apology a success.

For those who come to this book with some or much knowledge of the poet and his oeuvre, I have tried to provide not only summaries of the commonly accepted Slovene views of him, but critiques of them as well. I do this not out of a polemic sense, for it would avail Prešeren studies little for an outsider like myself to take issue with Prijatelj, Kidrič, Slodnjak, Kos, or Paternu, the most outstanding Prešeren scholars of this century. Rather I have hoped to make a modest contribution to Prešeren studies from my own, non-Slovene point of view, in the belief that the Slovene bard belongs not merely to his own nation, but also to the whole world community of those who appreciate poetry.

In attempting to reach both these audiences, my book seeks to balance the needs of the neophyte and those of the Slovenist. For the imbalances that inevitably occur, I ask my reader's indulgence.

I also beg the pardon of those who will look here in vain for a word about some of their favorite Prešeren poems. Of necessity I have had to leave out the treatment of several of the poet's works (none do I regret more than that of *Lepa Vida*), although I have tried to discuss all of his most important pieces. Where my selection comes to be judged nearsighted or incorrect, I ask only that my critic himself provide an analysis of the missing masterpiece, so that this introduction of Preš-eren to the English speaking world becomes as complete as possible.

Many reasons have prompted me to undertake this study of Preš-eren, but perhaps it is Sir John Bowring, the British Slavist of the early nineteenth century, who articulated my principal motive most elo-quently. What he wrote concerning Bohemian literature in the intro-duction to his *Cheskian Anthology* applies equally well to Slovene:

The virtues become more intellectual—the intellect more virtuous, by some-times travelling beyond the little limits of family, and tribe, and nation. It is most delightful and most improving to feel concerned in the well-being of those who are far removed from us—to hail them as part of the great family of man. To influence their felicity is the lot of but few—to rejoice in it and so to share it, might be the privilege of all.

In the course of writing this book, I have accumulated many debts to fellow Slavists and other friends. Some of these I hope I repay in the text and the notes, but to a few a special, separate note of gratitude must be offered here: to the University of Illinois' Russian and East European Center I am particularly indebted for support during the summers of 1977 and 1978, in order to use the outstanding resources of the University of Illinois Library; to the librarians of the Regenstein Library of the University of Chicago I owe many thanks for access to the splendid Slovene collection there; and to my own institution, Northwestern University, I am deeply grateful for the free time afforded me during the spring quarter of 1978 to bring this book into being. On a personal note, I have greatly appreciated the advice and encouragement of Professor Albert B. Lord, who read the manuscript and made several helpful suggestions. To Professor John F. Loud, who initiated the idea of this book, provided the framework for its realiza-tion, Twayne's World Authors Series, and painstakingly read and reread the text as both editor and friend, I am indebted literally beyond words. To Mrs. Natalie Hector, who typed the manuscript and in the process suggested numerous emendations in both style and substance, I owe my profound thanks. Finally, to Professor Rado L. Lencek, who first introduced me not only to Slovene, but, by his example, to the noble ideal of the scholar, I humbly dedicate this book.

HENRY R. COOPER, JR.

Northwestern University

Chronology

1800   Francè Prešeren is born, 3 December, in Vrba, Upper Carniola; the third child, first son, of Šimen and Mina Prešeren-Ribič.

1808   Leaves home to attend school; lives for a while with his uncle Jožef, a priest. Kopitar publishes his Slovene grammar.

1812   Goes to Ljubljana to continue his studies.

1819 (?) Begins to write poetry in German.

1822   Moves to Vienna and enters the Law Faculty of the University.

1824   Writes his first preserved text, "Letter to His Parents"; (?) begins to compose poetry in Slovene.

1825   Metelko publishes his grammar in the *metelčica*.

1827   Publishes his first poem, "To The Girls," in Slovene and German. Matija Čop returns to Ljubljana from teaching in Lwów.

1828   Receives his law degree and returns to work in Ljubljana; begins his close friendship with Čop.

1829   Initiates the unsuccessful affair with Maria Khlun of Graz.

1830   *The Carniolan Bee*, volume 1 is published, containing several of Prešeren's poems, including "Farewell to Youth."

1831   *The Carniolan Bee*, volume 2 is published, containing even more of Prešeren's poetry; the "Ljubljana ABC War" begins.

1832   Spends half a year in Klagenfurt preparing for legal examinations he does not do well on. *The Carniolan Bee*, volume 3 is published, containing his poetry. F. L. Čelakovský in Prague writes a review of the *Bee* and singles out Prešeren for praise.

1833   Čop publishes his articles on Slovene orthography and literature, thus ending the "Ljubljana ABC War"; the *metelčica* is banned. Prešeren falls in love with Julija Primic, 6 April.

1834   *The Carniolan Bee*, volume 4 is published with many of Prešeren's poems; "A Wreath of Sonnets" is published and causes a scandal. Goes to work in the law firm of B. Crobath in Ljubljana after having been refused permission to open his own practice. Meets Stanko Vraz for the first time.

1835   Prešeren's uncle Jožef dies. Čop drowns. Ljudevit Gaj begins to publish his Illyrian newspapers in Zagreb.

1836   Julija Primic's engagement to Jožef Anzelm von Scheuchen-stuel is made public; the poet's hopes are dashed; meets Ana Jelovšek. Publishes "The Baptism on the Savica."

1837   Emil Korytko arrives in Ljubljana and befriends Prešeren.

1838   Father dies.

1839   Korytko dies; Julija Primic is married; Prešeren's first child by Ana Jelovšek is born, but dies a year later. Korytko's folk collection, *Slovene Songs of the Carniolan People*, begins to appear posthumously.

1840   Prešeren and Andrej Smolè edit the Slovene classics. The poet is again refused an independent practice. Smolè dies.

1842   Mother dies. Ana gives birth to the poet's second child, Ernestina (d. 1917).

1843   The first Slovene-language newspaper since 1800 is published in Ljubljana, *The Peasants' and Artisans' News*, by Janez Bleiweis; Prešeren is not asked to participate in it.

1844   Kopitar dies. Jovan Vesel-Koseski publishes "Slovenia to Kaiser Ferdinand." Bleiweis publishes a new edition of the "Baptism."

1845   Health begins to fail; denies Ana's third child, Francè (d. 1855), is his; she leaves to live in Trieste. For the fifth time the poet is refused an independent practice.

1846   Is finally granted permission to establish his own law practice in Kranj. Publishes the anthology of his Slovene poetry (*Poems*, dated 1847).

1848   *The Carniolan Bee*, volume 5 is published after the revolutions of 1848 end the Metternich era; it contains a few of Prešeren's folk adaptations and the patriotic "Toast." B. Crobath dies. The poet tries to commit suicide.

1849   In total poverty Prešeren dies, 8 February.

1866   Stritar and Jurčič reissue Prešeren's anthology, reviving interest in him and initiating the "cult of Prešeren" in Slovene literature.

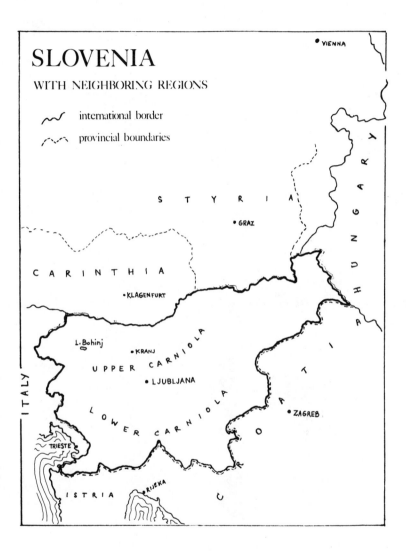

SLOVENIA

WITH NEIGHBORING REGIONS

∿ international border

∿∿ provincial boundaries

• VIENNA

S T Y R I A

• GRAZ

C A R I N T H I A

• KLAGENFURT

H U N G A R Y

L. Bohinj

• KRANJ

U P P E R   C A R N I O L A

• LJUBLJANA

L O W E R   C A R N I O L A

• ZAGREB

C R O A T I A

ITALY

TRIESTE •

I S T R I A

RIJEKA

C

CHAPTER 1

The Necessary Background

FOR a brief while, at the beginning of the nineteenth century, the capital of Slovenia was Paris, for Napoleon, sensing the strategic value of this headland of the Balkans, had wrested from Austria control of the area and annexed it to his empire. As a fitting designation for the new territory, he revived its ancient Roman name; he called it "les provinces illyriennes" ("the Illyrian provinces"). And like so many of his reforms, this one too was to live on long after his passing. Even when Austria regained control over the Slovene lands in 1813, the name Illyria remained, at times to bedevil and at times to encourage Slovenes, but always to remind them of a moment of unity in their long and divisive history.

The history of the Slovenes, a small nation—no more than 2.3 million worldwide—of Southern Slavs living on the westernmost salient of the Slavic world, stretches back to the sixth century, when the first groups of Slavic peoples began moving from their tribal homeland, north of the Carpathian Mountains, somewhere in today's Poland, south, toward the Adriatic Sea.[1] The initial Slovene settlement in the Eastern Alps encompassed a much larger territory than that which is occupied by Slovene speakers today, but over the centuries, under pressure from more numerous neighbors, the Slovenes retreated and consolidated into a compact body along the northern reaches of the Drava and Sava rivers. In the eighth century, when the Slavic migrations ceased, two of the most fundamental events occurred which were to shape all the rest of Slovene history: first, the baptism of Slovene princes, and eventually the entire populace, into the Western (Catholic) Church, and second, the loss of Slovene independence to the Franks.[2] For the next 1,100 years, until 1918, the Slovenes were to remain subjects of Germanic kings and bishops.

The succeeding several centuries witnessed two processes that arose from the conversion and conquest of the Slovenes and had a profound impact on their history and culture. The more insidious was the gradual settlement of Slovene lands by immigrating Germans, who slowly but relentlessly displaced the Slavic population or absorbed it. A natural phenomenon, really, given a political and racial cast only when heralded later as the infamous "Drang nach Osten" (Drive to the East), the movement of Germans into the Eastern Alps was probably perceived as a mixed blessing by the local inhabitants. On the one hand it meant a rise in the prosperity and sophistication of the area, at the price, on the other hand, of the native Slavic dialects and traditions. In the days before conscious nationalism, such a loss probably meant less than it would today.

The other process undergone by the Slovenes at this time involved their ever greater isolation from other Slavic speaking groups. Particularly as a result of the Magyar invasion of Europe at the end of the ninth century and the subsequent establishment of the Hungarian state in the Pannonian plain (the area roughly equivalent to modern Hungary), the Slovenes' natural and direct contact with the Slavs living there was eliminated, and a barrier to further contact with the Western Slavs—Czechs, Slovaks, Poles—and Eastern Slavs—the Russians—was erected. Furthermore, with the inclusion of the Croatian kingdom into the lands of the Hungarian crown (1102), an international border was set up between Slovenes and Kajkavian Croats,[3] another group of Southern Slavs whose language was very similar to that of the Slovenes. From this time on the Croats were to grow away from the Slovenes, both in terms of their culture, which became Magyarized, and in terms of their language, which came to share similarities with Serbian. Thus by the thirteenth century the Slovenes were isolated from the larger Slavic continuum, all the while being drawn more tightly into the orbit of the German states of Central Europe.

Eventually the Hapsburg dynasty secured control of all the territories in which Slovenes were living (by about 1457). Under a strong central government, the German-speaking Austrians were able to make even greater inroads in the Slovene lands. The language of government, commerce, and culture became exclusively German. (Latin of course was used in the church and some schools, and Italian was heard in the western and littoral regions of Slovenia, but elsewhere German predominated.) Only the peasants spoke Slovene, but their status in feudal Austria was so abysmally low that there could be no interest in their language.

One might think that by the middle of the eighteenth century the

Germanization of the Slovene lands would have been complete. Slovene could not be heard outside the marketplace. The Slovene area had been divided into six distinct Austrian provinces (Carniola, Carinthia, Styria, Gorizia, Trieste, and Istria, with a small group of Slovenes living in Hungarian territory as well), only one of which—Carniola—had a Slovene majority. Even the ethnic designation of the inhabitants had become moot: Slovenes who wished to avoid the German term "Winden" ("Wends") to describe themselves, had to make use of regional designations ("Carniolan") or phrases ("a Carinthian Slav") to point to their Slavic origin. But few sought to make even that minimal distinction.

CHAPTER 2

The Spiritual Situation

IF THE physical situation of the Slovenes was characterized by powerlessness, oppression, and exploitation, their spiritual situation fared no better. So long as worth was perceived as a function of size and might, the Slovenes, like other Slavic and European minorities, were condemned to insignificance. When in the course of the European religious revolutions of the sixteenth century the notion of worth changed to reflect the value of each soul in the struggle against evil, however, the standing of the Slovenes improved. Numbers became less important as every individual became vital to the new churches. No group was too small to escape the fervent attentions of the reformers. Eventually even the Slovenes were addressed in their own tongue by a Slovene apologist for Martin Luther. With that the spiritual and intellectual life of the Slovenes truly began.

Four principal figures helped to introduce and then spread Lutheranism among the Slovenes. In the process they laid the foundations of a Slovene Lutheran literature. Foremost among them is the father of Slovene letters, the first man to write in Slovene, Primož Trubar (1508-1586), an ordained priest, an early disciple of Luther, and a pupil of the humanist bishops Piero Bonomo and Pier-Paulo Vergerio. In 1550 he published in Tübingen *A Catechism* and *A Spelling Primer,* and from 1555 through 1577 he worked on and published a Slovene translation of the New Testament, various Protestant theological works, the Psalter, and hymns. In addition he attempted to regularize Slovene spelling and introduced the use of Latin (as opposed to Gothic) script for books.[1] His follower, Sebastijan Krelj (1538-1567), advanced these last reforms by further refining the spelling system and ridding Trubar's Slovene of its more egregious Germanisms. Krelj's work reached its culmination in the labors of Jurij Dalmatin (ca. 1547-1589), who in 1584 in Wittenberg published a Slovene translation of the complete Bible, which in its language and orthography was so successful that it survived even the Counter Reformation and was used by the Catholics. The fourth and last of the Slovene reformers was Adam Bohorič, who helped Dalmatin in his Bible translation and published also in 1584 in Wittenberg his most important work, *The Winter Hours*, the first grammar of Slovene. Here he laid down the principles of Slovene spelling that were to last until the 1840s; the system, named in his honor, was called "bohoričica." It, like the Dalmatin Bible and the memory of Slovene Protestantism (but not its substance), was the only thing to survive the re-Catholicization of the Slovene lands, which began in earnest under the Hapsburg emperor Ferdinand II in 1598 and was completed by 1628.

In the history of Slovene intellectual life, the next 150 years rank among the darkest. In this respect, Slovenia shared fully in the history of Central and Eastern Europe, where religious and civil wars devastated once vital regions. To be sure, there were occasional bright spots—in Slovenia the brightest of them all for the period was the publication of the first Slovene history, *The Honor of the Duchy of Carniola*, in German by Janez Vajkart Valvasor in 1689— but the impetus of the Protestant writers had definitely been lost. Once again German ruled, and creative impulses did not radiate from Slovene centers.

Only the enlightened despotism of two Hapsburg rulers was able to prompt a revival of interest among Slovenes in their language. Maria Theresa (who ruled from 1740 to 1780) and her son Joseph II (1780-1790) provided the necessary stability, prosperity, freedom, and encouragement for their subjects to indulge in national development. In the Slovene lands the Theresian and Josephian reforms aided the first hesitant enlightenment attempts at historiography (Marko Pohlin and Anton Tomaž Linhart), linguistics (Pohlin and Ožbalt Gutsmann), ethnography and folk literature (Leopold Volkmer, Baron Žiga Zois), education (Blaž Kumerdej), and belles-lettres (Linhart, Feliks Dev, and Valentin Vodnik). In all there may have been a hundred revivalists[2] seriously trying to create a sense of Slovene self-awareness in the late eighteenth century. By far the majority of them were clerical figures, and many of these of the "Jansenist" inclination.[3] Of all of them perhaps only two had a permanent impact on Slovene intellectual life, for they are still read today: Anton Tomaž Linhart (1756-1795) and Valentin Vodnik (1758-1819).

These two, under the guidance and with the support of their

Maecenas, Baron Žiga Zois (1747-1819), the reviver of the "Academy of the Industrious" (1781) and the promoter of the first Slovene newspaper, the *Ljubljana News* (1797-1800), were the precursors of Prešeren. Linhart founded the Slovene theater with his apt translations of Beaumarchais and Joseph Richter, and he informed Slovene nationalism with his two-volume history, *An Attempt at a History of Carniola and Austria's Other Southern Slavs* (1788-1791).[4] Vodnik, a priest, was the first writer of secular poetry in Slovene, an enlightened cleric whose interests were political and definitely revivalist. He went so far as to pen a poem, to the detriment of his later career, entitled "Illyria Revived" (1811), in honor of Napoleon and the founding of the Illyrian provinces.[5]

Thus by 1800, the year of Prešeren's birth, the spiritual situation of the Slovenes appeared more promising than at any other point in their history. The national revival had begun, based on the achievements of the sixteenth-century Protestant writers, joined to the rationalism of the eighteenth-century enlighteners. The movement was still not self-sustaining, however, as the decline in Slovene letters was only too clearly to show after the Austrian restoration.[6] A third cycle was necessary to achieve a fully vital Slovene culture. That cycle was to be initiated by the grammarian and antiquarian Jernej Kopitar, the professor of literature Matija Čop, and above all the poet Francè Prešeren.

CHAPTER 3

Prešeren's Life

A CONTEST was held in 1852 to write a poem commemorating
the life of Francè Prešeren (he had died 8 February 1849). The
winner was a young boy, Fran Levstik, whose entry was a heartfelt
elegy to a poet bedeviled by misfortune and grief.[1] Later Levstik
was to go on to fame as a poet in his own right, and to become
known in Slovenia as the cofounder, with Josip Stritar and Jožef
Jurčič, of the cult of Prešeren.[2] But even at this early date Levstik
had a profoundly accurate perception of Prešeren's life, which was
one of unremitting sorrows compounded of frustration, depression,
despair, and alcohol.

Anton Slodnjak, a modern critic of Prešeren, confirms Levstik's
insight: "Pessimism is Prešeren's most innate point of view and
arose doubtless from the experiences of his life and professional
disappointments."[3] In Slodnjak's biography of Prešeren, as well as
in all the others,[4] the reader comes quickly to understand the plight
of Slovenia's most outstanding writer: he possessed a Promethean
poetic spirit housed in flesh that yearned for the standard comforts
of his time. Again and again he was frustrated by the circumstances
of his life and location, the worst of all possible milieux, some say,
for an artist to have been born in.[5] He sought to resign himself to
his fate. Long fits of depression signaled his attempts to be
indifferent to his environment. But in the final analysis he could
never become sufficiently insensitive, for until the final years of his
life he would always respond anew to the stimuli around him. He
wrote, he worked, he even tried to love, and, when all else failed, he
fought off his innate morbidity with drink. Ironically it may have
been the very poetic spirit that bedeviled him which ultimately
enabled him to withstand his numerous misfortunes. For Prešeren
poetry seems to have been something like an outlet for a variety of
his frustrations—erotic, political, emotional. A connection exists
between the details of his biography and the products of his artistry.

21

Therefore we turn to the historical facts of Prešeren's life as a first
step in appreciating his poetry.

For the sake of convenience the life of Prešeren can be divided
into four parts: from birth to the completion of his formal education
(1800-1828), the period of his greatest poetic creativity (1828-1836),
the period of slow deterioration with spurts of activity (1836-1846),
and the period of complete deterioration (1846-1849). As any life,
Prešeren's is of a piece. What loss of integrity this four-fold division
entails is recompensed, I hope, in the final section, which seeks to
draw some conclusions from the biomaterial presented here.

I   1800-1828

The poet was born on 3 December 1800 in house number one of
the Upper Carniolan ("gorenjski") village of Vrba, north of Ljubljana. His household name was Frencè, and in the village his
family were referred to as the Ribič's. But he was baptized shortly
after as Franz (Slovene Francè),[6] and in all official matters he used
the clan surname Prešeren (spelled by the poet in several different
ways, the favorite being Preschérn). The third of eight children, he
was the first son of Šimen and Mina, well-to-do peasants, and his
parents' favorite child.[7] He was raised in an atmosphere of piety
and respect for learning. Though his father was illiterate, his mother
could read and write both Slovene and German, and she saw to it
that all her children, even the girls, learned to do the same. Family
life seems to have been serene: the children never wanted for bread,
and at least Francè was spared the normal menial responsibilities of
a child in a peasant household.[8] From the beginning he was singled
out for his intelligence, wit, and inclination to rhyming.[9]

The Prešeren clan boasted many educated members—the two
most favored professions were priest and lawyer. It was to one of his
learned relatives that Francè was sent for his education. In 1808 he
moved in with his uncle, Father Jožef Prešeren, in Kopanj, to begin
his studies. In 1810 he moved on to the primary school in Ribnica.
Here, while he was rooming with one of the masters of the school,
some profoundly moving experience befell him, the exact nature of
which remains unknown. Yet it was of such moment that Prešeren
recalled it on his deathbed.[10] The likely solution suggests that it was
here, sometime between his tenth and twelfth year, that he was
introduced to alcohol, the abuse of which in fact did kill him.[11] On
the other hand we should not exclude the possibly sexual nature of
the experience,[12] although Prešeren himself seems to contradict this.

As Ana Jelovšek, his mistress of many years, told her daughter, Prešeren's illegitimate child Ernestina, Prešeren claimed to have been initiated into the mysteries of sex in his sixteenth year.[13] Since reasons exist to question the accuracy of Ana's memory on this score, however,[14] the incident that occurred at the Ribnica school must remain, perhaps forever, a mystery.

Little else about his adolescence is mysterious. In 1812 he was sent to Ljubljana to the next class, and there he was to stay until the fall of 1821, making of course occasional visits to his parents and his uncles, especially Jožef. Ljubljana during the first two years of his stay was still the capital of the French "Illyrian provinces." Therefore he studied French and Latin as well as German (Slovene was not an official language, indeed was not even taught, in Ljubljana at this time). Later, in 1818-1819, he took Italian as an elective subject. In all his studies he was an excellent student consistently placing first, second, or third in every class. His services were constantly in demand as a tutor on account of his high grades.[15]

In Ljubljana friendships were made and habits confirmed which were made to remain with Prešeren throughout the rest of his life. He had no need to practice frugality, for with his earnings as a tutor and the generous allowance his uncle Jožef sent him, he had money enough to squander, which he did. With friends he frequented several of Ljubljana's 160 or so beer and wine shops—one for every 75 of the city's approximately 12,000 residents (men, women, and children!)[16]—and even founded with them a mock "Students' Wine Consumption Commission."[17] Success in studies came easy; Prešeren did not have to burn any midnight oil. But success in society was more difficult. He was acquainted with many people, but befriended by only a few: the two most important of his friendships were with Matija Čop, his senior by two years and an equally bright student, and Andrej Smolè, the son of a famous Ljubljana businesswoman. Physically he was not very attractive. He walked with a stoop and stuttered a bit; he forced himself to speak slowly to conceal his speech defect.[18] Although he presumably could afford the expense, he did not dress very elegantly. These facts, coupled with his humble background, made him less than appealing to city girls of refined homes.[19] And his lack of success there cast a small but enduring shadow on his youth.

While Prešeren was somewhat restrained in the company of his male friends, with whom he nonetheless drank amply and regularly, he seems to have been more outgoing with women, especially those

he met in the inns he frequented. With these, the daughters of the
tavern owners or simply the serving girls, particularly the young
ones, he enjoyed talking and joking. He liked especially "to speak
of erotic things, and then in a witty, double-meaning way."[20] All
through his life he preferred almost prenubile girls—Ana Jelovšek
was only fourteen when he met her, and at fifteen and a half she
was pregnant with their first child.[21] While he gave himself the airs
of a rake, one analyst at least feels he may have been chaste well
into his thirties. The outlet for his fantasies were words and gestures,
but never, apparently, actions.[22]

Of Prešeren's political inclinations in this first period of his life it
is impossible to say anything concrete. With Kidrič we may specu-
late that he was probably neither an Austrian chauvinist nor a
political revolutionary.[23] Rather, like so many other of his fellow
citizens in the Austria of Prince Metternich and the Holy Alliance,
he was content to leave politics to the politicians and to pursue the
comforts of the "Biedermeier," the triumphantly bourgeois period
of tranquillity, later of stagnation, that followed the Napoleonic
Wars. As for religion, the poet never shared his mother's inclination
to great piety nor her desire for him to become a priest. By 1824 in
Vienna, away from the Jansenism of Ljubljana, he had definitely
become a "lapsed" Catholic.[24] Though he never renounced his
faith, and despite the fact that he returned to the fold a few days
before his death, there is no reason to think of Prešeren for the bulk
of his life as any more than a cultural Catholic.

In 1821 he moved to Vienna to finish the last year of the lyceum
and then enroll in the Law Faculty of the Vienna University. His
decision to pursue law, not theology, met with disapproval from his
parents, but his uncle Jožef, understanding better perhaps the
impossibility of forcing a calling, agreed to continue Prešeren's
allowance. For one year Prešeren secured a job as a master at
Friedrich von Klinkowström's "Educational Institute," a bastion of
Austro-Catholic conservatism which meted out to the sons of the
nobility discipline and religion in heavy doses. The poet might have
held onto his position for more than a year, had he not been caught
giving "undesirable," i.e., classical and Renaissance, reading matter
to one of his students, the young Count Anton von Auersperg, who
was later to become the mildly seditious poet "Anastasius Grün."[25]
Prešeren was not inconsolable at the loss of his position. Indeed,
judging from the one extant letter to his parents, dated 24 May
1824, the poet's first preserved writing and one of his rare prose

texts, we might conclude that his time in Vienna was spent pleasantly and without major incident.[26]

During the school holiday in the summer of 1824 he returned to Ljubljana to visit family and friends, and was smitten with love for Zalika Dolenc, the approximately twenty-year-old daughter of a Ljubljana tavern keeper. She would appear to be Prešeren's "first Laura,"[27] that is, the first of his erotic attachments to stimulate him to write poetry.[28] Zalika, certainly no stranger to the advances of her father's customers, rejected Prešeren out-of-hand. The memory of that rejection, as well as the infatuation he experienced then, were to enter the poet's earliest works, particularly "The Water Sprite,"[29] in the first version of which the heroine is even called Zalika. As in all of Prešeren's subsequent amorous writings, the intent of these early works seems less to celebrate the beloved girl than the fact of Prešeren's love. The poet's lyric "thou" is rarely of greater consequence than his "I."

By 1828 Prešeren had passed all of the examinations leading to the law degree and had prepared a dissertation, which he defended successfully in March of that year.[30] Before returning to Ljubljana to look for a job, he spent a summer on the Moravian estate of Count Emmanuel Dubský, the father of one of his pupils in Vienna. When he did return to Carniola at the end of the summer, he found a rather tense situation at the home of his parents, where Mina, the only one of his sisters to marry, had begun with her new husband to split up the family holdings. Although he himself had not lived in Vrba since 1810, Prešeren must surely have regretted the dissolution of his happy childhood home with its pleasant memories. And as he took up residence in Ljubljana later that year, with home and school now forever lost to the past, and the prospect of a career and a home of his own beckoning in the future, he must have also had the sense of the closing of one period in his life and the opening of another. What was in fact to follow was the most productive decade of his life.

Before examining this period, however, we must expand somewhat on the information above concerning Prešeren's first writing. As early as 1819, that is, while he was still studying in Ljubljana, Francè may have begun to compose verse in German for his own amusement and that of his friends.[31] He may even have written in Slovene at that time, as many of his colleagues, encouraged by Franc Metelko, the first professor of Slovene at the Ljubljana lyceum, had done in the early 1820s.[32] Or his "love" for Zalika may have been the stimulus to his first Slovene verse. In any event, by 1825 or 1826 he had a sufficient quantity of poems of acceptable quality that he decided to show them to Jernej Kopitar, the most learned and respected Slovene of the time, who was censor for Slavic and New Greek books in Vienna. The scholar advised the poet to let the poems be for a while, then to rework them. Prešeren, frustrated in his attempts to polish them, decided instead to burn all but three texts.[33] On 12 January 1827 another poem, "Dekletam" [To the Girls], appeared anonymously in the Ljubljana German-language weekly together with the poet's own German translation of it.[34] This, plus the three surviving poems of the early collection, are all that remain of Prešeren's juvenilia. But right from the beginning it is evident that Prešeren represents a far higher level of poetic accomplishment than any of his Slovene predecessors. As Stritar claims, Prešeren took almost no time to find the right tone and produce, unlike Vodnik or any others, perfect lyrics.[35]

II *1828-1836*

On 1 September 1828 the poet began to work for the law firm of Dr. Leopold Baumgarten of Ljubljana as a "praktikant," or unpaid assistant. According to Kidrič's description of him, he was of medium height (170 centimeters or 5 feet 7 inches), slender but solid, with stooping shoulders, a broad head, and a long face. He appeared far more refined than an ordinary peasant's son. Inclined to be sulky, he smiled more often than he laughed, but at twenty-eight he was essentially honest, sincere, and innocent.[36] Evidently the young doctor did not lack completely the admiration of the fairer sex. Before 1833 he was known to have an interest in Rezika Krištofbert (sixteen years old), Marička Metkin (thirteen-fourteen years old), Jerica Rotar (fifteen years old), Ana Endlicher (nineteen years old), Marija von Mullitsch (twenty-five years old), an unidentified Ljubljana woman, an unidentified Klagenfurt woman, and, perhaps the most serious of them all, Maria Khlun, a wealthy German woman of Graz whom he almost married.[37] For the most part these girls were simple, young, and flighty, but the relationship with Khlun was of a different sort altogether. They met in 1829; the sister-in-law of a highly placed magistrate and an heiress, she had much to offer Prešeren. At the beginning they wrote to one another often, but by 1832 the poet had dropped his end of the correspond-ence and, after one last attempt to see him, Khlun likewise gave up on him. Kidrič reports that she died sometime shortly thereafter.[38]

One can detect little ardor on the poet's part, and even less regret after the affair, for "the German" (as he is reported to have referred to her).[39] Never again, however, was Prešeren to be so close to marrying as he had been in 1829-1830 with Maria Khlun.

The poet's legal career entered upon a different track when in 1829 he left Baumgarten to work for Anton von Scheuchenstuel, the Ljubljana imperial counsel, once again as an unpaid assistant. He found government service no more rewarding, though, and after two unsuccessful attempts to win an "adjutum" ("financial aid"), he returned to Baumgarten in 1831 as a "koncipient," or paid legal clerk. There he stayed until 1834, when he accepted a similar position with the firm of Dr. Blaž Crobath, a drinking companion and friend in whose family Prešeren was always welcome. There he would remain for the next twelve years.

Professionally it must have been frustrating for the poet to serve in positions so far beneath his ability and education. To overcome this, he moved for four months in 1832 to Klagenfurt, to prepare for an examination that would allow him to establish himself in an independent practice. (The number of law firms in Austria was limited by law; an attorney had both to pass an examination and be licensed for one of the available openings before he could practice.) Despite his earlier brilliant academic record, however, Prešeren received only the lowest passing grade on this important examination ("satisfactory").[40] His chances for an independent practice were sharply curtailed as a result. His first application for one, which he submitted in 1832 despite his poor standing, was rejected. Indeed he would not succeed until his sixth attempt, in 1846, by which time the accumulated frustration of five rejections had deprived him of any love for his profession, or any enthusiasm for an independent position.

Only in friends and in poetry could the poet boast of success in this period, and each seemed sufficient to keep him relatively happy. His most important friend, with whom he spent endless hours discussing literature and for whom he even moderated his drinking, was Matija Čop.[41] After teaching stints in Rijeka, on the Dalmatian coast, and in Lwów, in the Austrian partition of Poland, Čop had returned to Ljubljana in 1827 to teach. Eventually he was made librarian of the Ljubljana lyceum, a post to which he was innately suited thanks to his love for books, his voracious reading habits, and his command of thirteen languages.[42] Though somewhat lazy and himself a twice-rejected lover,[43] Čop had the profoundest

effect on Prešeren's poetry. To him perhaps more than to any other
of the revivalists the credit is due for generating the great burst of
Slovene cultural activity in the 1830s, which was to result in a self-
sustaining Slovene cultural movement.

Prešeren's other close friend in Ljubljana at this time was Andrej
Smolè. In 1827 Smolè had left provincial Carniola to broaden his
horizons in London and Paris. When he returned in 1831, he was
like a breath of fresh air in the stuffiness of the Austro-Slovene
Biedermeier. Prešeren was particularly attracted to the dashing
Smolè for "his broad nature, his Dionysian flights, his Bohemian
life-style, his idealism and his good heart."[44] They were drinking
partners, collaborators, confidants. After Smolè's untimely death in
1840, Prešeren took in his illegitimate son, eventually giving the
boy a job in his law firm.

Beyond these few friends, the poet had only one other affection:
poetry. In 1829 he penned one of his most famous and perfect
works, "Farewell to Youth."[45] At the same time he cooperated with
five other young Slovene poets to launch a Slovene literary almanac,
the *Carniolan Bee*, under the editorship of Miha Kastelic, a friend
of his and fellow poet. Thanks to the mediation of Čop, who was on
good terms with both the provincial governor, Joseph Schmidburg,
and the major of Ljubljana, Janez Nepomuk Hradecky, the *Carniolan Bee* succeeded where so many other attempts had failed. Its
first issue was allowed by the censor to appear in 1830 and was
received very warmly by most of Carniola and the Slovenes of the
surrounding provinces.[46] Three of Prešeren's poems, including the
"Farewell to Youth" and "The Water Sprite," were printed in the
issue; they easily outshone all the other contributions.

Seeking to maintain the impetus of the first volume of the *Bee*,
Kastelic, Čop, Prešeren, and others brought out in quick succession
volumes 2 (1831) and 3 (1832). To both of these Prešeren contributed. In each case his were far and away the most sophisticated
poems in the collections, and his alone enjoyed enduring success.
Unfortunately plans for volume 4, which originally was to have
appeared in 1833, were frustrated by two events of cardinal importance which took place that year.

The first of these was the so-called "Ljubljana ABC War." In
February 1833 Čop published in the *Illyrian List*, the Ljubljana
German-language paper, a translation and commentary of a fulsome
review of the *Carniolan Bee* by František Ladislav Čelakovský, the
Czech enlightenment figure. As a result, Čop and Prešeren became

directly involved in a polemic which had been going on in Slovenia since 1831. Conflicting personalities aside, the essence of the "War" involved the replacement of the standard Slovene "bohoričica" spelling system with the new "metelčica," developed in 1825 by Franc Metelko, which included Cyrillic letters in a basically Latin-letter alphabet. Čop and Prešeren opposed the "metelčica" on aesthetic, historic, and linguistic grounds, and succeeded by the end of the year in having it excluded from all schools where Slovene was taught. But they paid dearly for their success, for Kopitar and his minions, supporters of the "metelčica," saw to it that the fourth volume of the *Carniolan Bee* would encounter troubles with the censorship. Although they could not ban it altogether, they were able to delay it. It was finally published only in 1834. The following volume suffered an even greater delay, however, appearing only after the abolition of the censorship in Austria, in 1848.

Prešeren responded to the "War" with unwonted sarcasm. To be sure he had shown himself to be a fine and biting satirist in his earlier poetic statements on the subject of literature and writing,[47] but in his "Literärische Scherze in August Wilhelm von Schlegels Manier" 1833,[48] [Literary Jokes in August Wilhelm von Schlegel's Manner,] he grew quite strident. He accused Kopitar of having plagiarized his famous grammar of 1808 from Baron Zois and of improper liberties with a "maiden," that is, Carniolan literature. The poet seems almost to have lost control of himself. To this he may have been driven by a review of his poetry written by Joseph Burger in February 1833 for the *Illyrian List*.[49] Burger wrote that Prešeren's poetry "offended morality." This charge the Jansenists were later to pick up and apply with special vigor to Prešeren's erotic poetry. Prešeren must have been grievously offended by this prudery, the more so because he was just then undergoing the most highly erotic experience of his life.

On Easter Eve, 6 April 1833, in the Church of St. John the Baptist at Trnovo, a borough of Ljubljana, the poet caught sight of Julija Primic, the seventeen-year-old daughter of a wealthy but stern Ljubljana matron. Precisely like Petrarch five hundred years before him,[50] he fell helplessly in love with her, although there is nothing to indicate she reciprocated the feeling. She became his Laura, the source of his poetic inspiration even when, in fact especially when, he realized that he had no chance of winning her. Julija was a pretty young woman.[51] Her dowry was large and her education, though minimal, was adequate to her station. Her mother, Julijana, kept

Julija on a tight rein and was forever wary of fortune hunters and would-be seducers of her daughter. The Primic home was the frequent refuge of the Ljubljana Jansenist clergy and was even graced on occasion with the episcopal visits, though he was not a Jansenist himself, of Bishop Anton Alojzij Wolf, who was reputed to have an eye for devout but beautiful women.[52] From all available evidence, Julija and her mother epitomized the Germanized Ljubljana upper bourgeoisie of their time in superficial culture, showy piety, arrogance, and spiritual bankruptcy. What could the poet see in her? If he had known her, probably little; but the fact is he did not know her at all. She functioned for him merely as the embodiment of his erotic fantasy. As Prijatelj concludes, "Julija gave his ideal a real name," but little more.[53]

The result of this encounter of the poetic sensibility with the woman he felt personified beauty and love was, of course, poetry. A similar reaction had occurred before, in "Prva ljubezen" [First Love, 1832], "Ljubeznjeni sonetje" [Love Sonnets, 1831-1832], and "Sonetje nesreče" [Sonnets of Unhappiness, 1832],[54] under the impact of some unrecorded Laura. This time, however, Prešeren reached the height of his poetic ability. He composed the work for which he is best known in and out of Slovenia, "Sonetni venec" [A Wreath of Sonnets], which was published in a special supplement to the *Illyrian List* on 22 February 1834. The "Wreath," basically an Italian poetic form never so successfully practiced by its developers as by its Slovene imitator, was like a bomb dropped on the placid social life of Ljubljana,[55] not only because of the consummate artistry of the text, but because the poet had dared to name his love in print. For Prešeren, the results were disastrous.

In his "structural biography" of Prešeren, Boris Paternu locates the beginning of a serious internal disharmony afflicting the poet in the period immediately following the publication of the "Wreath."[56] The long process of "demythologizing" his love for Julija began as he came to understand that he had lost her forever. At this point he also began to suffer career anxieties. He moved to a new position in Dr. Crobath's law firm, after failing to get one with the imperial counsel.[57] He made a second, hopeless attempt at obtaining for himself an independent practice. In all his disappointments he had few consolations to fall back on. If possible, Julija was colder than before because her mother had increased her vigilant watch over the girl and restricted all her movements. The Prešeren household in Vrba had definitely come apart the year before, and the poet's mother had taken up residence with the poet's brother, a priest in Klagenfurt. Only Čop, with his literary insights and sure friendship, offered the poet a refuge from the furies of unrequited love and public notoriety. And occasionally, in this year and the following, Prešeren had the opportunity to meet with important literary and social figures of the day: Janez Vesel (later to be known as Jovan Vesel-Koseski), the composer of the first Slovene sonnet; Karel Hynek Mácha, the greatest Czech romantic poet; Stanko Vraz, the East Styrian Slovene, whose interest in Slovene literature was double-edged; and others.[58] Apparently these meetings afforded the poet a small measure of enjoyment.

The following year, 1835, was not to treat Prešeren any more kindly than had 1834. In quick succession three tragedies befell him which left the poor man in a distraught state bordering on suicide. First, his favorite uncle Jožef died. Then his second petition for an independent practice was officially rejected, with every indication that he should hold out no hope for a different treatment of his application in the future. And, on 6 July 1835, Čop drowned, presumably as the result of a stroke, while swimming in the Sava River.[59] A fourth misfortune befell him as well, for his Julija was secretly betrothed to Jožef Anzelm von Scheuchenstuel. But the poet and the world were spared knowledge of the match until 1836, when the news was finally made public. The three tragedies, and especially Čop's sudden death, were sufficient, however, to drive the poet into deep depression, so deep in fact that he had to be ordered by a judge to finish the work he had begun in probating his deceased friend's estate. When he regained some of his composure, he began to drink again. He put on weight, turned grey, and became more negligent of his appearance.[60] In 1836 he and his sister Katra, who had been Jožef's housekeeper, took an apartment together. Residing thus for them was a matter of necessity, in that Katra was without resources. She drank too,[61] so that one can imagine the poet's home life was anything but wholesome. Shortly after the events of 1835 and 1836 Prešeren developed dropsy, which became chronic and which, joined to his incipient cirrhosis, would ultimately help to kill him.[62]

This period of Prešeren's biography would not be complete without mention of the two literary works which were prompted by the death of Čop. The first, "Dem Andenken des Matthias Čop" [To the Memory of Matthias Čop, 1835],[63] is a German-language elegy written almost immediately after the event. One wonders why the poet chose to bemoan the cruel loss of his friend in German; the answer may lie in his desire to inform Europe at large of the passing of a great talent, and to do this he wrote in one of the international languages of the day. The other response to Čop's death was slower in coming but of far greater moment in the history of Slovene literature. Prešeren wrote the miniature epic, "Krst pri Savici" [The Baptism on the Savica, 1836],[64] with a prefatory sonnet, "Matiju Čopu" [To Matija Čop] in which he dedicated the work "to the dear shade of my friend."[65] The "Baptism" forms, with "A Wreath of Sonnets," the other great peak of Prešeren's poetic production. It assured his reputation as the first poet of the Slovenes (though this was still a position without much honor in the 1830s) and it entered him into the lists of Slavic poets who had written or would write national epics: the Russian Alexander Pushkin, *Evgenij Onegin* (1831); the Pole Adam Mickiewicz, *Pan Tadeusz* (1834); the Croat Ivan Mažuranić, *The Death of Smailaga Čengić* (1846); and the Montenegrin Serb Petar Petrović Njegoš, *The Mountain Wreath* (1847). As his hero Črtomir, so too Prešeren at the end of the "Baptism" entered a new phase of his life. The period of greatest creativity was over, a period of lessened creativity about to begin.

III   *1836-1846*

The hopelessness of his love for Julija Primic and the devastating loss of the only friend who had taste and education enough to appreciate him gradually undermined the poet's desire to write. The next decade of his life shows the poet turning away from original composition. Instead he occupied himself with compilational activities—the first mention of a collection of his poetry was made in 1836; by 1846 *Poezíje dóktorja Francéta Prešérna* [The Poems of Doctor Francè Prešeren] saw the light of day[66]—and undertook matters like publishing and editing, which were really peripheral to his literary activity. Under the repeated blows of family difficulties and professional frustrations, he gave himself up to alcohol more and more. And even when he found a measure of personal happiness in his unofficial union with Ana Jelovšek, he was not stirred to write by it.[67]

Even without his personal troubles, the whole tenor of the times was working against Prešeren. By 1835 the opposing trends represented by the "metelčica," with its Jansenist supporters, and the *Carniolan Bee*, with its romantic, modernist orientation, seemed to have canceled one another out. The cultural field was left open, then, to ethnographers, who collected and adapted folk songs, and to teachers, who wrote didactic tales for school children. The censorship after the appointment of Anton Stelzich in 1834 grew so strict that only religious and legitimistic works could readily appear; Prešeren had difficulty getting even his inoffensive elegy to Čop passed.[68] And the political situation despite the death of Francis II in 1835 and the accession of his son, the weak-minded Ferdinand I, remained completely moribund. As a result of the latter's political and fiscal conservatism, economic stagnation spread throughout the empire; it may have been the principal cause of the Ljubljana bourgeoisie's turning from thoughts of a Slovene revival and concentrating their efforts once again on their own affairs.

If a certain depression had set into the Slovene cultural scene at this time, the same could not be said of Croatia, where under the vigorous leadership of Ljudevit Gaj new cultural initiatives were being undertaken. The most important of these was the Illyrian Movement, in essence a drive to increase the cultural and political awareness of the Croats,[69] but couched in terms of the union of all South Slavic peoples in a single cultural continuum. In 1835 Gaj founded a Croatian-language newspaper and literary supplement which he printed in the old, Hungarian-based orthography with Zagreb dialectal features. By 1836 he switched his publications to the new "Czech orthography" (so called because it was based on the Latin alphabet expanded with the help of diacritical marks invented by the Czech religious reformer Jan Hus in the fifteenth century), and the Štokavian dialect, which was spoken by all the Serbs and many of the Croats. Unfortunately, the Štokavian version of Serbo-Croatian was farther from Slovene than the Zagreb dialect of Kajkavian Croatian had been. But Gaj was willing to forsake closer ties with the Slovenes, who were few and oppressed, for the sake of union with the Serbs, who were not only far more numerous but also politically quasi-independent. In any event, he felt sure the Slovenes could accommodate themselves to "Illyrian," an eclectic South Slavic literary language he and his followers sought to develop on the basis of Štokavian Serbo-Croatian.[70]

To the end of persuading the Slovenes to consider the use of "Illyrian," Gaj's chief spokesman, a Styrian (i.e., Northeast) Slovene, Stanko Vraz, came to Ljubljana in January 1837 to speak with Prešeren. Vraz, a friend of Prešeren's,[71] wanted the poet to abandon his Carniolan Slovene and adopt "Illyrian" for poetic purposes. Furthermore, he urged the acceptance of the Czech orthography in

Slovene as well. On both scores Prešeren was opposed.[72] Vraz left Ljubljana disappointed and probably embittered, for after this he drew closer and closer to the Croats, eventually abandoning his native tongue to write poetry in Serbo-Croatian, a language he unfortunately never quite mastered. Prešeren successfully defended the nascent Slovene literary language, which he himself had almost single-handedly created. But in the process he seemed to be gambling on the chances of Slovene standing on its own against the assimilation pressures of the Austro-Germans. And he antagonized some Slovenes, like Vraz, whose defections could have dealt a death blow to the Slovene revival.

Fortunately for Prešeren, help was proffered by the Western Slavs. The arrival of two Polish exiles in Ljubljana served to signal the start of a new pro-Slovene drive. The day after Vraz left Ljubljana, in January 1837, Emil Korytko and Bogusław Horodyński arrived from Lwów, where they had been arrested for having a copy of Adam Mickiewicz's messianic treatise, *Books of the Polish Nation and Pilgrimage*. Prešeren met them at his employer, Dr. Crobath's, house, where they often came because Crobath's wife, herself Polish, was quite solicitous for her exiled countrymen. Still mourning the loss of Čop, Prešeren soon found a substitute in the energetic Korytko who, perceiving the need for an accurate collection of Carniolan folk songs, immediately undertook to compile one with Prešeren's help.[73] Eventually they collected enough for five volumes. These they intended to print in the new Czech orthography, which they may have seen both as a way of accommodating the Illyrians and fending off their further demands.[74] But Korytko died suddenly in 1839, at the age of twenty-six; his work ultimately found its way into the hands of Jurij Kosmač and Miha Kastelic (the former editor of the *Bee*), who published it as *Slovene Songs of the Carniolan People* in 1839-1844, without the cooperation of Prešeren.

The death of a friend also deprived Prešeren of the fruits of his labor in another area. The poet and Andrej Smolè decided to attempt a Slovene-language newspaper, the first of its kind in Ljubljana since the folding of the *Ljubljana News* in 1800.[75] At first they thought merely in terms of a Slovene supplement to the new German-language paper begun in Ljubljana in 1838 by Leopold Kordesch, entitled *Carniolia*. But with the rejection of that idea by the editor, they set out to found a full-fledged Slovene organ which would act as a forum for political and social news as well as cultural and belle-lettristic offerings. They chose their titles deliberately:

Ilirske novice [Illyrian News] for the paper itself, and *Ilirski Merkur* [Illyrian Mercury] for the cultural supplement, again to make use of some of the interest in the Illyrian Movement while at the same time stealing the wind from the Croatian Illyrians' sails.[76] But before Smolè could get final government approval, he too died.[77] Again Prešeren was left bereft by the death of a friend, and this time his last close one. When in 1843 a Slovene newspaper was begun in Ljubljana by Janez Bleiweis, a veterinarian, Prešeren had no hand in the undertaking, in part because he had not been asked to, and in part because he was falling into increasingly deeper apathy and alcoholism. In a letter to Vraz in which he criticized the paper and its editor for the poor quality of the Slovene and for their ignoring him, he also added: "I work seven hours for Dr. Crobath in order to drink for two hours at that old ——— Metka's."[78]

Death and illness took their toll among all of Prešeren's family and friends, making the period 1836-1846 certainly the saddest in his life. In addition to his own dropsy, the poet's employer, Dr. Crobath, became at this time an alcoholic. Prešeren's other much-loved uncle, Jakob, died in 1837, followed shortly by the poet's father in 1838. The poet's first child by Ana Jelovšek, Rezika, born in 1839, died in 1840. And in 1842 his mother died, predicting—correctly—that Prešeren would be the first of her children to follow her in death.[79] By the early 1840s the poet had lost most of his family and all his close friends; he was left with Crobath, who abetted the poet's own alcoholic tendencies; Kastelic, whose role in Čop's drowning Prešeren could never clarify;[80] and, for better or for worse, Ana Jelovšek.

Ana, the poet's mistress from 1837 until 1845, never lived with Prešeren. Although at times they would see one another every day, they always maintained separate apartments.[81] And what their relationship lacked in domesticity, it also lacked in tranquillity; their years together were marred by arguments, separations, and misunderstandings. They probably started off on the wrong foot, for it seems Prešeren's interest in Ana was tinged with his still lively feelings for Julija Primic. Ana, whose godmother was Julija's mother, had lived as a ward in the Primic house from 1830 to 1836, when she left to work as a nurse for the Crobaths. Kidrič speculates that Prešeren, by paying attention to a lesser personage of the Primic household, may have been trying to embarrass Julija, whose engagement to Jožef von Scheuchenstuel had been announced precisely then, in the winter of 1836-1837.[82] No evidence of Julija's displea-

sure can be adduced, however, and it is a fact that Prešeren's earlier
years with Ana, through the birth of the first child, were relatively
happy.[83] In the final analysis the poet may have been attracted to
Ana for her youth, her good looks, and her simple background, not
for her value as a tool of revenge.

Ana eventually bore the poet three children. In giving up the first
to relatives to be cared for, she provoked a split with the poet which
worsened when the infant died in 1840. Their reconciliation did not
occur until the spring of 1841 and it resulted in the birth of another
daughter, Ernestina (died 1917), who has left behind a valuable if
somewhat biased memoir of her father.[84] Ana, who was a willful
woman unable to learn from her mistakes, also sent Ernestina to the
country to be cared for by relatives. Moreover, she provoked
Prešeren further by appealing to his acquaintances and others to
persuade him to marry her. He resolutely informed her in 1843 that
he would not wed, and even suggested that she learn a trade so that
after his death she would be able to support herself and her child.[85]
He remained true to his word not to marry her even after the birth
of a third child in 1845, whom Ana named Francè and registered as
a Prešeren, though she had no right to do so. Prešeren seems to have
doubted the paternity of his "son," who died in 1855, six years after
his father. In any event, he and Ana were by that time farther apart
than ever. On his deathbed she appealed to him to recognize legally
the children as his own. Only at the final moment did he agree; he
left them and Ana all his money, which however amounted to very
little.[86]

Ana and the poet spoke German together. He thought her
Ljubljana dialect was too execrable to be Slovene.[87] He did not
write any poetry for or about her, with the possible exception of
"Nezakonska mati" [The Unwed Mother, 1845].[88] On the other
hand he did write several ballads and other pieces—sonnets he
wrote only for Julija and his early loves—under the impact of his
"last Laura," in Kidrič's phrase, one of the daughters of the tavern
keeper Metka Podboj, at whose establishment the poet spent long
hours. The "Laura" in question was probably Jerica Podboj, a
seventeen-year-old whom the poet courted unsuccessfully in 1841.
In 1842 she married an English industrialist, David Moline, who
had factories in Slovenia. With that the amorous side of the poet's
life comes to a close, at least as far as later researchers have been
able to discover.

Little remains to mention about the poet in this third period of his life except for his professional frustrations and his publication of the *Poems*. After the failure of his second application for an independent practice—he was notified officially in 1835—Prešeren had to wait until 1840 before he could apply again. Changes in official policy had reduced the already limited number of independent practices and Prešeren, with his poor showing in the legal examinations of 1832, his reputation as a "Freigeist" ("free spirit" or "rebel") and his affection for the bottle, could hardly have expected to compete successfully with the other candidates. Thus his third application was rejected as were his fourth of 1843 and his fifth of 1845. By this time his health had become seriously impaired through chronic dropsy and drinking. Ana had left him and moved to Trieste after the birth of Francè.

Undoubtedly without any hope, Prešeren submitted yet a sixth application to the authorities in the spring of 1846. This time the regular Ljubljana police chief was on leave and his replacement, Edvard Suchanek, a Czech, deliberately gave Prešeren such a glowing recommendation—out of consideration for what the poet had already suffered—that the commission accepted the poet's application.[89] On 22 July 1846, Prešeren was notified that he had been awarded the right to open a practice in Kranj, northwest of Ljubljana.

Coincidentally, on the very same day the poet also received word that his anthology had been approved by the new censor for Slavic books in Vienna, Franz Miklosich.[90] Miklosich, who had replaced Kopitar after the latter's death in 1844, made only the slightest alterations in the poems, so that the integrity of Prešeren's collection was maintained. A run of 1,200 copies was then commissioned from the Ljubljana publisher J. Blaznik, The book appeared in December of 1846, but the title page was imprinted with the date 1847.

Around the beginning of October 1846 Prešeren, his sister, and Smolè's illegitimate son left Ljubljana for Kranj. Sometime just before he had effected a reconciliation with Ana, even agreeing in principle to adopt the child Francè, though he continued to maintain it was not his.[91] His life seemed to be entering a new phase, one hopefully free of the hindrances of the preceding decade. But, as Paternu points out, the disintegrational process at work in Prešeren had already gone too far.[92] By 1845 depression and drinking had begun to predominate; career and poetry, even with the impetus now given them in 1846, were never again to occupy the poet wholeheartedly. As a result, the last period of his life was

characterized by inactivity and increased morbidity. Only the rate
at which Prešeren was deteriorating accelerated.

IV   *1846-1849*

Kranj, the capital of Upper Carniola, was in 1846 only a fraction
of the size of Ljubljana, numbering in all some 2,000 souls.[93] It had
no schools above the elementary level, no book stores, no theaters,
only taverns, churches, and provincial ennui.[94] Even for a vigorous
person life would have been difficult there; for Prešeren it was fatal.
The outlays necessitated by his move and establishment of a practice
strained his slender financial resources to their limit. He was
hampered in the cases he did get by his inability to concentrate his
efforts for any length of time. He alienated the powers that be in
Kranj by pleading cases against ecclesiastical figures. What were left
of his friends lived a long coach ride away in Ljubljana. And with
the death of his friend and legal mentor Dr. Crobath in the summer
of 1848, even the number of his Ljubljana friends dwindled to
practically zero.

The heady political situation of 1848, when revolutions were
breaking out all over Europe and even Slovenia was granted the
removal of certain onerous taxes and the abolition of the censorship,
left Prešeren untouched. Some critics have tried to paint the poet in
this last period of his life as a "progressive" whose "humanism and
democratism" were revealed in his work at this time.[95] But there are
precious few facts on which to base such assumptions; from the
evidence that is available it would seem safer to conclude that
Prešeren in Kranj was an isolated, inconsolable, and rather pathetic
figure. He no longer wrote, and by the end of 1848 he could not
even walk. He even failed when, in midsummer, he tried to commit
suicide.[96]

By November he was compelled to take to his bed, never to rise
from it again. He carried on with some of his responsibilities from
there, however, and even kept abreast of developments in the
newspapers. He was, for example, displeased with a report in the
Peasants' and Artisans' News of January 1849 which said that he
was seriously ill. With more humor than he had evidenced for many
a year he notified the editors that he was healthy enough yet to read
about himself in the paper. They happily printed a retraction of
their story.[97] But a few days later the inevitable occurred. He made
his peace with Ana and received the final consolation of the church.
And at about eight o'clock in the morning of 8 February 1849 the
poet died.

In the end we are left with a picture of the poet as a failure, both professionally and artistically.[98] Were it not for our current appreciation of his poetry and the role his sorrowful biography played in shaping it, little in his life could lay claim to our attention now. Prešeren's biography without his poetry is the pedestrian tale of business ups and downs, family spats, bad health, a quiet death at home in bed.[99] He lacked the dash of Byron or Mickiewicz, the access to power of Pushkin or Njegoš, the refined spleen of Lermontov or Słowacki. Even in his most amorous moments— moments of fantasy more than reality—he was hardly the embodiment of an Alpine Don Juan, though he might have liked to be. The life of the Slovene poet is redeemed in the eyes of the generations that have followed him only in the two slender volumes that comprise his collected works. Perhaps more than other romantic poets, Prešeren's enduring fame and vitality derive exclusively from what he wrote and not how he lived.

CHAPTER 4

Prešeren and the Intellectual Life of Slovenia

A BIOGRAPHY of the poet would not be complete without an assessment of his impact on the Slovene intellectual world, particularly of the 1830s. That world was tiny, especially after the passing of the first generation of revivalists: Vodnik and Zois both died in 1819 and Janez Primic in 1823. Those who were left—Kopitar, who resided in Vienna from 1808; Jakob Zupan, Matevž Ravnikar, and Franc Metelko in Carniola; Urban Jarnik in Carinthia; Valentin Stanič in Gorizia; Peter Dajnko and Anton Murko in Styria—had become by the 1820s, if they were not that way before, Austro-Slavist in politics, Jansenist in religion, and conservative in their literary tastes. For the most part they eschewed the new romanticism that had become so popular in England, France, and Germany. They looked to Viennese models for inspiration. Above all they preferred the tract, the textbook, and the pamphlet to the poetry whose "immorality," they felt, threatened the stability of altars and thrones.

While they were in the majority, the Slovene cultural conservatives did not, however, have a complete monopoly over opinion in the Slovene provinces of Inner Austria. Another group, under the leadership of Matija Čop, and including Andrej Smolè, Miha Kastelic, and of course Prešeren, promoted a rather different point of view. Without revolutionary intentions, they favored a Slovene, rather than Austro-Slavist, kind of patriotism. Their literary program was cautiously romantic, more akin to Goethe's than Byron's. They opposed the benighted Jansenism of some of their critics, but respected religion in general and Roman Catholicism in particular as the faith of their nation. In a word, this party sought the maximum exercise of Slovene intellectual and artistic freedoms within the restrictions of Metternich's tightly controlled state. It probed the limits imposed by altar and throne, but it would be incorrect to think it sought in any way to unsettle, let alone overthrow, them.

A third group also had a profound impact on the Slovene intellectual elite in the period from the mid-1820s to the beginning of the 1840s, but they were not Slovenes themselves. They were Poles, Czechs, Slovaks, and Croats, that is, the other Slavic groups ruled at this time by the House of Hapsburg. The Poles and Czechs encouraged the development of an independent Slovene culture, either by example—Mickiewicz, Mácha—or by actions of their own—Korytko, Čelakovský, Palacký, even Dobrovský. The Slovaks and Croats, on the other hand, offered a radical solution to the question of Slovene development. They advocated the absorption of the Slovene lands into a larger South Slavic ("Illyrian") entity, for the sake of the survival of Slavs as a whole and their ultimate achievement of cultural and political independence. To this group belonged Kollár, Šafařík, Gaj, and the Slovene-become-Croat Vraz.

In a sense, Prešeren was not at home with any of these groups. At one point or another he satirized them all in his poetry, even Čop.[1] Yet they all played a profound role in the formation of his poetic opus, either by exasperating him so that he would fling one of his poetic bolts at them, or encouraging him to launch out in new directions, to try a new genre or meter. Thus their activities must be understood in order to appreciate the poet and his poetry. We start with Čop first, for he made the greatest contribution of any to Prešeren's poetic development.

I *Matija Čop (1797-1835)*

We can gain some idea of Čop's influence on Prešeren if we realize that Prešeren wrote his best poetry from 1828 to 1835, the period of his closest association with Čop; that the more time passed after his friend's death, the less Prešeren wrote and wrote well; and that the last major poem Prešeren was to compose was the Slovene-language elegy to Čop (in 1846).[2] The Slovene commentators of the Čop-Prešeren relationship have often disagreed on the precise extent of the friendship.[3] But the facts speak for themselves; no one else had more direct contact with the poet, nor a greater impact on his life or his work than did Čop.

Prešeren in his Slovene elegy called Čop "a giant of learning,"[4] and with good reason. Despite his frequent moves and limited resources, Čop as early as 1828 had a personal library containing some 2,000 volumes.[5] He was devoted to reading: he went to all the book shops in whatever city he visited, he wrote about literature in all his letters, he discussed it with all his friends.[6] In Prešeren's phrase, Čop "devoured books,"[7] and in any language; according to Kidrič he knew twelve in addition to his native Slovene: Greek, Latin, English, French, Spanish, Portuguese, Italian, Provençal, German, Polish, Russian, and Serbo-Croatian.[8] By means of letters and visits he was in direct contact with many of the brightest minds of the day, particularly in the Slavic world: Kopitar, Čelakovský, Palacký, Jungmann, Šafařík, and other scholars in Galicia, Bohemia, Austria, Croatia, and of course the Slovene provinces.

Like the poet's, Čop's personal life had not been the happiest. He experienced rejection at the hands of the woman he loved, and he never recovered from it.[9] Professional frustration likewise dogged him: his three posts, in Rijeka, Lwów, and Ljubljana, could not be called prestigious. Although in 1830 he found a position as librarian of the Ljubljana lyceum, a post which in some ways was ideal for his talents and tastes, he always aspired to more. Had his life not been so tragically shortened, he may very well have won a teaching position one day in Vienna or Northern Italy. Wherever he lived he seemed to be at home, rapidly making friends, learning the local language, becoming acquainted with the literary personalities of the area. In short, Čop's very life epitomized the sophisticated internationalism he advocated in literature.

All of what we know of Čop's literary views comes from three sources—his correspondence with friends, his very few publications, and the remembrances of him by his followers, especially Prešeren.[10] Čop's writings, published and unpublished, do not bulk large. A somewhat diffident scholar, he produced little: a chapter for P. J. Šafařík's revised version of *The History of the Slavic Language and Literature* (first edition, 1826), on Slovene literature, which was, however, not published until 1864; a German translation of F. L. Čelakovský's Czech-language review of the *Carniolan Bee* (in the *Illyrian List*, 9 February 1833); plus his own commentary on the state of Slovene literature and the validity of alphabet revision [16 and 23 February]; and three other brief but penetrating articles of his on the "Ljubljana Alphabet War" (running from March to July 1833 in the *Illyrian List*).[11] Even when we add his letters to his friends Savio and Prešeren, and correspondence with Kopitar, Čelakovský, and others, the whole of his extant writings amounts to a very slender volume indeed. But they reveal quite clearly Čop's thinking on the nature of literature and its role in the national life.

Čop drew on both literary praxis and theory to inform his views. His tastes in poetry and prose were incredibly wide-ranging, if we are to judge on the basis of the books in his library. But he preferred his contemporaries, the romantics, above all the rest, particularly Goethe, Mickiewicz, Manzoni, Byron, and Scott.[12] He was also moved by the classical Italian writers, placing Dante especially at the head of his pantheon,[13] and by the Spanish writers of the Golden Age, Juan Boscán and Garcilaso de la Vega. In matters of literary theory, analysts have identified in Čop's statements on the subject ideas drawn from Charles Batteux, Friedrich Bouterweck, and the brothers August Wilhelm and Friedrich von Schlegel, especially F. Schlegel's *Discussion About Poetry* (1800). Particularly in regard to the Schlegels has the matter of Čop's indebtedness been a contested point in Slovene criticism: some (e.g., Žigon)[14] have argued that the *Discussion* forms the basis of Čop's, and consequently Prešeren's, literary viewpoint, that it was in fact accepted as the program of a "Čop Academy," a Slovene version of the Italian Renaissance accademia of literature and art. Others (e.g., Slodnjak)[15] dispute the importance of the Schlegels in general. They claim there was no fixed program, but that Čop culled his ideas from many sources, modifying them creatively in the process.

Čop did share with the Schlegels many general perceptions of the world of letters. These shared viewpoints are of critical importance not only in understanding Čop, but Prešeren as well. They are, in Boris Paternu's formulation of them, as follows: that poetry is the foundation of a cultured nation, therefore for a nation to be cultured, it must cultivate poetry; that it must do so in its own language, the one distinctive feature which most clearly sets off one nation from another; that art as a whole, made up of numerous national components, is, however, international, and that the art of one nation can and should have an impact on that of other nations; that of all the art forms represented in the world in their time, the Italian stand higher than the rest, and therefore represent a suitable source upon which less developed nations might draw.[16] While the first two of these perceptions served, it would seem, as unarticulated understandings in Čop's and Prešeren's poetic views, the last had a more direct, practical application in the Čop-Prešeren relationship. For Čop evinced a great fondness for problems of form and genre, which oftentimes eclipsed his interest in the content of a poem.[17] Even more than the Schlegels, the Slovene was a scholar of literature, he knew its various European manifestations well, he had firsthand experience with English blank verse, Italian terza rima, the Serbian "deseterac," Polish Alexandrines. Authorized, as it were, by the cosmopolitanism of the Schlegels' literary pantheism, that is, that all creation is one, Čop seems to have conceived of himself as the importer of European, especially Italian, poetic forms into Slovene. And even if he did not actually assume an active literary role in the awakening of his land, he served as a source of literary information for Prešeren on all the varieties of European poetic expression and their suitability for use in Slovene.[18]

It is equally important to consider where Čop's views differed substantially from the Schlegels'. For one, the Slovene rejected the rigidly Catholic bias of the Austrian brothers. For another he was much more keenly aware of the Slavic romantics than were the Schlegels. Kollár, Mácha, and Mickiewicz offered Čop ideas especially on nationalism which the Schlegels ignored.[19] Čop held Byron in particular in much higher esteem than did the Schlegels, whose perception of the English poet was colored by their pietism.[20] Most important, Čop and Prešeren both drew heavily from sources other than the Schlegels for the theoretical underpinnings of Prešeren's poetic practice. As Slodnjak has repeatedly pointed out,[21] Čop and Prešeren's "program," insofar as we can speak of a clearly elaborated plan for the development of a modern, secular Slovene literature, drew on native Slovene resources (Kopitar, Metelko, the earlier Slovene writers); other European literary theorists (Bouterweck, Batteux); Čop's own insights, which were in turn based on his direct appreciation of all the major literatures of classical and modern Europe; and Prešeren's personal views, which for his part derived from his firsthand knowledge of German, Italian, and classical poetry. The Schlegels' contribution, though not inconsequential, was by no means the only one.

More important, however, than Čop's introduction of new poetic forms for use in Slovene or his placing his vast knowledge and good taste at the disposal of his friend, was his conviction that Slovene was worthy and capable of development. In his February 1833 articles he admitted quite bluntly that Slovene was the least developed of the Slavic literatures, with the possible exception of Lusatian Sorbian,[22] that it was difficult if not impossible to write in a cultured way in the language, and that this situation was deplorable and should be remedied. Not every one agreed with him. On the contrary, Kopitar and some of his followers treated Slovene almost as a museum piece, that is, with great respect but with unwillingness to see any changes occur in it. Even Prešeren cultivated his poetic talents in German as well as Slovene, nor did he condemn the Slovenes who wrote poetry in German.[23] Čop, perhaps more than any of the rest of his fellow Carniolans, wanted to win educated Slovenes away from German by the creation of a rich artistic literature in Slovene, on par with German and other European literatures in content and form. He hoped to create a mass of literary consumers who would guarantee the continuation of a Slovene-language culture.[24] These hopes were validated by Prešeren's first poems, for Prešeren somehow managed to fashion out of the stylistically undifferentiated peasant Slovene of his time texts that were subtle, readable and—most important—enjoyable. The symbiotic relationship of the two men—neither could have accomplished as much without the other—laid the foundations of Slovene secular poetry. In the process they created a readership which ultimately formed, in Anton Slodnjak's phrase, the "backbone" of the emergent Slovene nation.[25]

To attribute such importance to Čop in the formation of Prešeren's poetic views does not detract in any way from the latter's attainments as a poet.[26] If we consider the monumental achievement of Prešeren in creating through literature a Slovene literary language in the incredibly short span of ten years (1827-1836) and of blending antique and modern styles in a language which knew neither, then we might reasonably posit that he had help. And the help he had was Čop, with whom he could talk, from whom he could receive information, to whom he could show his poems for criticism, and with whom he could undertake what in that time must have seemed thankless, almost hopeless tasks: the arousal of scarcely self-aware Slovenes to nationhood, and the replacement of German in their social life by Slovene.

II   *Jernej Kopitar (1780-1844)*

With Čop, the most educated Slovene of the first half of the nineteenth century was Jernej Kopitar.[27] Unlike Čop, he was a prolific scholar, not without political interests, and constantly in contact with many intellectuals of his day. In 1808 he moved from the provincial backwater that was Ljubljana to Vienna, the heart of the Austrian empire. In short order he acquired power, as censor for Slavic and New Greek books (1810), prestige, as the author of several important philological studies, pretensions, as the heir of Joseph Dobrovský, the father of Slavic studies (died 1829), and a reputation for arrogance and pride.[28] Where Čop's relationship with

Prešeren had been warm and supportive, Kopitar's relationship with the poet was destructive from the start.

Their first significant contact seems to have occurred in the winter of 1825-1826, when Prešeren showed Kopitar a collection of his Slovene poems.[29] As a result of that meeting, Prešeren burned most of his early work, but it may be the poet was sorry he had followed the censor's advice, especially when it became evident in the 1830s that Kopitar was not well disposed to Prešeren's poetry in general. In fact, the poet mentions twice in his correspondence[30] that Kopitar held a lower opinion of his poetry than it perhaps deserved. In any event, by the early 1830s Prešeren's confidence in Kopitar was gone. Indeed, a rift had opened between the two men.

That rift was soon widened by the Ljubljana ABC-War, the "child's illness of a young literature," as it has been termed.[31] Unlike real wars, it was both brief (1831-1833) and bloodless. Its opening salvos were fired in a series of pro and con articles by Joseph Burger and Jakob Zupan entitled "The Cyrillization of the Slovene Alphabet."[32] The repercussions of these articles, however, were felt far beyond the classrooms which were the ostensible targets of alphabet reformers and alphabet conservatives alike. In fact, the "child's illness" was really a matter of life or death for secular literature in Slovene.[33] At issue were two very different perceptions of culture and cultural development, not merely orthography. Čop and Prešeren shared one view, which has come to be considered the "progressive," "democratic," "humanist," or, perhaps most neutrally, "liberal" one; Kopitar and his disciples held the other, which likewise has subsequently been labeled "Jansenist," "obscurantist," "Austro-Slavist," or simply "conservative."

It was Kopitar who had initiated the movement which led ultimately to this war. In his first book, *A Grammar of the Slavic Language in Carniola, Carinthia, and Styria*, written many years earlier (1808), he had called for a new Cyril, who, like his namesake of the ninth century, would create a second Cyrillic alphabet, close to the Latin, but with special adaptations—i.e., new letters—so that the languages of the Western and Southern Slavs could be spelled simply and uniformly.[34] Behind Kopitar's call lay two hopes: that related languages with identical writing systems might eventually coalesce into a single literary idiom in which all the Western and Southern Slavs could write; and that such a coalescence of Slavic peoples, particularly Catholic Slavs, would occur around a Viennese center, ending perhaps in the unification of those Slavs in one

Austro-Slavic state.[35] Kopitar was not a revolutionary, however; he believed in the slow evolution of languages and political movements. He foresaw the passing of many generations before the first fruits of Slavic unity would ripen. His intent here as elsewhere in his early writings was merely to initiate the processes, which, he felt, would then continue in a nautral, organic way.

Nor was Kopitar an obscurantist, although such is his reputation among some scholars to this day. As Ivan Prijatelj rightly indicates, Kopitar's program hewed to the rationalist-humanist line propounded by Baron Zois's circle in Ljubljana (of which he had been an integral part, as the baron's protégé).[36] This circle in turn derived its principal ideas from the French Enlightenment and those German thinkers, such as Adelung and Schlözer, who combined in their work patriotic fervor with scientific precision. Particularly in two beliefs which he held all his life did Kopitar reveal his indebtedness to these sources. One concerned "linguistic purity": the purest, and therefore the most prized language, was the one with the fewest nonnative elements (i.e., foreign borrowings); thus the best language was that of the simplest and most isolated peasants, and not the transmogrified dialect of the cities or the universalized, factitious idiom of art.[37] Second, all such "pure" languages had both an innate integrity and the right to exist and develop naturally. This belief he applied with particular vigor to his native Slovene.[38] Though a paradox clearly existed between his call for the amalgamation of all Slavic languages into one and his defense of the independent existence of Slovene, Kopitar never seemed particularly troubled by it, for amalgamation lay for him in the far distant future, while protecting and developing Slovene stood as an urgent call of the here and now.[39]

Working from these principles, Kopitar was the first to establish a norm for Slovene, thus giving later writers, including Prešeren, a stable linguistic framework within which to work. Beginning in 1813 he rendered aid and advice to Vuk Stefanović Karadžić who, despite the vigorous opposition of some ecclesiastical figures, reformed the Serbian alphabet and Serbian orthography, codified the grammar, collected folk songs, and began a Serbian lexicon. Kopitar discovered and published in a scientific format various monuments of Slavic antiquities, including the Freisingen documents, the oldest Slovene text. And even though his later years were troubled by acute paranoia, he continued to write, encouraging other Slavic philologists to do the same. Unfortunately, in the matter of choosing disciples he was not as successful as he had been in the other endeavors of his scholarly life.

Of the three followers in particular who played an important role in Kopitar's life—Father Jakob Zupan, Bishop Matevž Ravnikar, and Franc Metelko, all of whom disappointed their mentor in one way or another in the end—only Metelko had an impact on Prešeren's life as well. While Kopitar opposed the romantic poetry of the 1820s for the danger it implied to church, state, and the morality of the young, Metelko was not so adamantly against it. Indeed, in his lectures on Slovene—which Čop may have heard at the Ljubljana lyceum but Prešeren did not—he encouraged the writing of poetry and the use of Italian models with, however, a Slovene national content.[40] In 1825 he published his grammar, *A Basic Course in the Slovene Language in the Kingdom of Illyria and Neighboring Provinces*,[41] in which he proposed a new alphabet for Slovene, based on Kopitar's suggestions. The "metelčica," as it came to be called, replaced the Slovene digraphs (zh, sh, ſh) with single letters adapted from Cyrillic; by means of invented letters it made vowel quality explicit (open versus closed; reduced versus full). The result was hardly satisfactory, however, for the reform did not go as far as Kopitar had wished, nor was the alphabet aesthetically or practically acceptable. Still, sensing an opportunity to capitalize on the new market in textbooks, especially after the school authorities admitted the "metelčica" into Slovene-language schools in 1828, several writers began to produce books for publication in the new alphabet. These first literary efforts in the "metelčica" were all stillborn, and have since been mercifully forgotten by history.

Although they did not engage in any polemics during the first five years of the "metelčica," Čop and Prešeren did undertake to prevent the further erosion of Slovene literary standards from even the modest levels set by Vodnik, Dev, and Linhart, by promoting the publication of the first volume of the *Carniolan Bee* in 1830. Thus the *Bee*, a poetic almanac printed in the old "bohoričica" spelling, must be seen as a direct reaction to the "metelčica" and its attendent literary expressions; furthermore, it can be construed as the first exchange between the two sides in the ABC War.

More exchanges followed quickly. Beginning in 1831 Prešeren, venting his accumulated frustration with the linguistic purists who claimed literary worth for peasant agricultural tracts, penned some of his sharpest satires against Ravnikar, Metelko, and Kopitar. The most brilliant of these, "Nova pisarija" [The New Way to Write,

1831][42] and "Apel in čevljar" [Apelles and the Cobbler, published in 1833],[43] heated up the ABC War to the point where, in 1833, it turned into open polemics between Čop, writing articles in the *Illyrian List*, Prešeren, composing his devastating "Literary Jokes in August Wilhelm von Schlegel's Manner,"[44] and Kopitar, who wrote "A Word Concerning the Ljubljana ABC Conflict."[45]

The central issue of the polemics of February through July 1833 concerned *context*. That is, in which context was Slovene culture to be further developed, the Austrian or the Slovene? To develop within the context of Austria implied the continued association of the Slovene lands politically and culturally with Vienna. Kopitar's ideal was a Slovenia both Catholic and Austrian in allegiance; its culture would be traditional, based on the peasants and the villages; its principal claim to national uniqueness would be its language, a Slovene "purified" of Germanisms, used by the folk for its simple needs.

To develop within a Slovene context on the other hand implied a radically different perception of Slovene needs. Austria was irrelevant for Čop and Prešeren, and religion was unimportant too. The peasants were not the chief object of their interest, but rather the Germanized, educated city populations of the Slovene lands. The future of a Slovene nation rested with these people. Without educated speakers, there would be no Slovene and no real Slovene culture. If their Germanization proceeded any farther, however, Slovene would remain an inchoate Austrian dialect. But win them away from German, convince them of the expressive possibilities of their mother tongue and then induce them to use it—Slovene might then grow into the sophisticated instrument of a viable nation.

To Čop's eternal credit he understood clearly that the underlying issue in the ABC War was not alphabets, but context, not how Slovene was to be written, but rather how it was to be used and by whom. And he perceived that in the talent of Prešeren he possessed the greatest proof of Slovene's potential for sophisticated expression. In his estimation the resources of the language in the 1830s were still too circumscribed for its use as a medium of social and scientific intercourse. But brilliant poetry, which requires after all only one genius but which can have an immediate impact on broad masses of people, could carry the day. As he himself wrote (in German, of necessity): "Although it is scarcely possible, as the result of certain conditions, to consider the development of other areas of knowledge in our local language, still nothing prevents our *poets* from competing gloriously with poets of the other Slavs."[46] Prešeren was able to compete successfully not only with the other Slavs (who posed no immediate threat to Slovene), but with the "metelčica"-writers as well, whose lack of talent would have doomed Slovene letters to mediocrity. The happy and fortuitous combination of his genius with Čop's insights assured the eventual development of a Slovene capable of intellectual rigor and artistic beauty, a language, in the view of the Schlegels and their followers, befitting a full-fledged nation.

As a result of the ABC War, the "metelčica" was banned, first from Slovene schools at the end of 1833, then from official use at the beginning of 1834. Čop and Prešeren had found an unlooked-for ally in their struggle against the alphabet: Bishop Wolf of Ljubljana, who had a long-standing dislike for the Jansenists, quite happily cooperated in eliminating their alphabet from public life.[47] The last book in the "metelčica" was printed in 1835, and with that the Alphabet War came to an end.

The victory of Čop and Prešeren also strengthened the hand of those Slovenes who sought unity in the other Slovene provinces. Carinthian Slovenes, who had remained "loyal" to the "bohoričica" script during the heyday of the "metelčica" in Carniola,[48] were once again united to the central tradition in matters of orthography. Styrian Slovenes, who had been beguiled briefly by visions of their own literature written in their own alphabet, the "dajnčica," also returned to the central tradition, though somewhat later. In the case of both Carinthia and Styria, however, writing systems were not the principal motive for renewed interest in the Carniolan situation: poetry was. Thanks to the *Bee* and especially Prešeren's poems in it, the central Slovene speech area could lay claim to precedence not only in numbers, but now in the level of cultural attainment as well.[49] As Anton Murko, the Styrian author of the *Theoretical-Practical Slovene Language Teacher for Germans* (1832), wrote by way of introduction to two of Prešeren's poems which he had included in his grammar: "I cannot resist citing here the following two poetic texts which. in originality, true 'Sloveneness' ['echte Slowenität'], poetic worth and yet general comprehensibility, stand out as a model of how one *can* and *should* write in Slovene. Both are taken from the *Carniolan Bee*, which appeared in Ljubljana, and bespeak the superiority of the rest of the journal's contents."[50]

Čop and Kopitar both grew silent after 1833, Čop first by choice and then, in 1835, in death; Kopitar because he withdrew more and more from the Slovene cultural arena, which had become so inimical to him. He was successful, as censor, in delaying the publication of the fourth volume of the *Bee* until 1834. But for the most part he came to focus his attentions elsewhere. As Prešeren wrote to Čelakovský in 1836:

The patriarch Kopitar has presented the Slavic world with the *Glagolita Clozianus.* We were hoping that he would make a gift of a copy of it to his fatherland's library, but that has not happened, so Kastelic has ordered a copy. He still spurns us, or to express ourselves more correctly, he has turned his gracious visage from us. He maintains salvation can be found in only one name. Indeed, we are of the opinion that there are many Apostles. The zealous enthusiasm which . . . reigns among the Czechs, fills us with joy and the hope for a better future for the Slavs; we fear only lest our nationality collapse before then.[51]

The interaction of Kopitar and Prešeren had led, then, to a fundamental reorientation of Slovene culture, away from the deadening Austro-Slavism of the well-meaning "patriarch," toward the more vigorous Slovene-centralism of Prešeren and Čop. The poet and his friend had successfully navigated the fragile bark of reborn Slovene culture past the Scylla of provincialism.[52]

III   *Illyrianism and the Western Slavs*

Like his contemporary, the Russian poet Alexander Pushkin, Prešeren too never crossed the boundaries of the empire in which he lived. Indeed, his only "foreign" travel seems to have been to Moravia during the summer of 1828. Otherwise his movements were restricted to the Slovene provinces, and Vienna with its environs.

On the other hand he maintained written contact with other parts of the Hapsburg realm and, most important, felt the pulse of movements elsewhere in the empire. In addition to events in Slovenia (discussed above in reference to Čop and Kopitar), the Slavic revival in the Czech lands and Slovakia, Polish romanticism, and the Illyrian Movement in Croatia all touched upon his life and his writing. These forces were personified for the poet in his three friends, F. L. Čelakovský, Emil Korytko, and Stanko Vraz, so that this last section on Prešeren and the intellectual life of Slovenia must concentrate on his ties with each of these.

While it is important to remember that Pan-Slavism "arose as a defensive movement of the Western Slavs"[53] and that Illyrianism,

its South Slavic offshoot, was little more than a program for a
Croatian national awakening,[54] it is equally essential to keep in
mind that both these movements rendered special service to the
Slovenes too. As Rado Lencek has pointed out, linguistic Pan-
Slavism bore within itself the seeds of a contradiction[55] by promoting on the one hand the development of any and all Slavic literary
languages while calling on the other for an amalgamation of them
into one, or alternatively four, literary idioms for use by all Slavic
writers.[56] The effects of this contradiction are nowhere more evident
than in Prešeren's career. For until 1837 the Slovene poet benefited
quite clearly from the support of the Slavic revivalists and their
interest in promoting even fledgling Slovene letters, but after that
year he had to endure their attempts to undermine the very
literature he had created.

The revival of Czech nationhood had been carried on successfully
for four decades when F. L. Čelakovský, the Bohemian poet of
substantial reputation, undertook to introduce to his Czech readership the first poetic fruits of the Slovene national awakening. In
1832 he wrote a very favorable review of the *Carniolan Bee*,
volumes 1-3 (1830-1832) for the *Journal of the Czech Museum*. In it
he singled out Prešeren's poetry for special mention. This review he
sent to the poet, who responded to his first international notice with
a warm note of thanks in Slovene to Čelakovský, Palacký, (the
Czech historian), and "all Czech friends of the Slovene language." [57]
Čop translated the review into German and published it, together
with his comments, in the *Illyrian List* in February 1833, which, as
we have seen, touched off the final battle of the ABC War.

It is clear from his two other letters to Čelakovský—both written
in German—that Prešeren and his friends relied upon the Czechs
for moral support in the struggle against Kopitar and the Jansenist
critics, as well as for practical support in the matter of printing
books in Prague, where the atmosphere was less restrictive.[58] The
poet even sought solace from his Czech friends when his Slovene
critics had seized the cultural initiative and his greatest friend Čop
had been taken away.[59] In all Čelakovský sought to oblige him.
Writing to Čop in 1834 the Czech poet had the following encouragement to offer him and Prešeren: "The Carniolans, whose language in my opinion possesses even more charm, should not allow
themselves to be shamed by the Croats. . . . Dr. Prešeren must
write, write and then again write more poetry—in Carniolan, of
course." [60]

Prešeren never met Čelakovský personally, but he did have the opportunity to meet with another Czech, Karel Hynek Mácha, Bohemia's greatest romantic poet, during the latter's stop in Ljubljana on 29 August 1834. The evening, which turned out to be quite merry,[61] may have resulted in Prešeren's hearing some examples of Czech romantic poetry recited to him by Mácha, in particular the Czech sonnets of Jan Kollár (1793-1852),[62] whose most famous work, *The Daughter of Sláva* (1824), the poet had till that time read only in excerpts, and those in English translation.[63] In both form and content, Kollár was to have a direct impact on Prešeren's poetry.

Kollár, the Slovak Protestant pastor from Budapest, was, like Prešeren, indebted to the group of romantic thinkers who had worked at the beginning of the century in Jena, especially the brothers Schlegel. Their romantic point of view Kollár expressed most vividly in his poetry, particularly the massive *Daughter of Sláva*. For example, he espoused a dual love for his fiancée Mina and for his Slavic nation:

> Mina or country—choose, and choose but one.
> My hand—tore out and broke in twain my heart—
> My country! Mina! Each shall have a part.[64]

This intertwining of the amorous and the patriotic, more particularly the tension between the two, as the poet desires to love both one and the other with equal ardor, may have influenced Prešeren in the formulation of "A Wreath of Sonnets," where a similar bifurcation can be found.[65] The love of the poet for his "Laura" embodied his abstract love for his nation; love for the nation ennobled his personal affection for the lady. In both Kollár and Prešeren the favorite romantic passion, love, was augmented and embellished with a peculiarly Slavic awareness of nation.

Yet a fundamental difference existed between the two poets' perceptions. The Slovak poet, who wrote in Czech and lived in chauvinistic Hungary, considered as his nation not merely the poor and oppressed Slovaks, but all the Slavs from the Elbe to the Pacific, and the Adriatic to the White Sea. All Slavs, and not just the small nation of Slovaks, were to stand up to the Hungarian demands for assimilation. Prešeren had no such global ethos. For him the Slovenes alone, only a million strong, were nation enough. In that much more limited context he sought to elaborate his feelings on love and country.

Until 1837 this discrepancy in national identification between Kollár and Prešeren did not play any significant role. On occasion in his letters Prešeren would complain of the carelessness with which other Slavs treated the Slovenes,[66] and even the indolent Čop had been moved by Šafařík's total ignorance of things Slovene to write a chapter on Slovene literature for his revised *History*. But before the publication of Kollár's major scholarly work, *Concerning Literary Mutuality Between the Various Branches and Dialects of the Slavic Nation* (1837), the issue had remained subordinate to other more pressing problems of the day. Only when Kollár had issued a definitive call for the restriction of all Slavic literary expression to the four major Slavic literary languages did the critical distinction between allegiance to Slavdom or Slovenia assume major importance in Prešeren's mind.

Of all the Slavic groups only the South Slavs possessed no clearly superior dialect which could serve as a ready-made vehicle for all of them to write in. Hence Kollár hedged his call for South Slavic unity by using the stylish but ambiguous term "Illyrian," whose meaning could be made precise, he felt, at some future date. Since he was more a poet than a scholar and was not well informed about South Slavic, and particularly Slovene matters,[67] the term "Illyrian," which at least enjoyed some currency in the circle of Ljudevit Gaj in Zagreb, seemed to suffice for his larger purposes. Other theorists could be found to flesh out the real implications of an "Illyrian" literary language for the South Slavs.

Gaj, who had befriended Kollár in 1830 and informed him on South Slavic matters, became the first of the "Illyrians." And Stanko Vraz, a Slovene from Southeastern Styria, followed him as another. As early as 1829, a few years, that is, after the initial Slovene reforms by Metelko and Dajnko, Gaj had begun his work on reforming Croatian orthography by adapting Czech diacritical marks to a simplified Latin alphabet. His purpose, quite clearly, was more than linguistic, for in reforming he hoped also to bring Dalmatian, Slavonian, and Zagreb Croats closer to one another. Given the revivalist and reformist trends among the Serbs, Gaj had every hope of extending his reforms south to them, reaching even as far as the Bulgarians, and north to the Slovenes.[68]

The headiness of Gaj's wide-ranging schemes for South Slavic unity attracted quite a following, mostly in Croatia, but also in part in Slovenia.[69] Despite the passive opposition of Prešeren[70] and outspoken criticism by Kopitar, who called Gaj's diacritics "Bohemian flyspots," some Slovenes thought they perceived the wave of the future in Gaj's activities. Chief among these "Slovene renegades," to use Prešeren's term,[71] was Stanko Vraz.

Vraz wavered many years before committing himself to Gaj's Illyrian Movement. Unsuccessful in his native Styria—he had an embarrassingly poor school record there[72]—he approached Prešeren during his first visit to Ljubljana in 1834. He sought to effect a compromise with Prešeren, whom even then he recognized as the greatest living Slovene poet, so that elements of his Styrian dialect (some desinences, a somewhat different vocabulary) would be included in Prešeren's Upper Carniolan dialect. Prešeren resisted this request, preferring to stay with his natural mode of speech, even though Vraz made it quite clear he found Carniolan Slovene difficult to understand.[73] Vraz left Ljubljana frustrated, to seek his fortunes with Gaj in Zagreb. In January 1837 he returned to Ljubljana a second time, once again to interest Prešeren in a linguistic compromise involving Slovene dialects. This time too Prešeren rejected his plan, and with that the entire Illyrian and Pan-Slavic scheme for amalgamation of Slavic literary languages. In the clearest statement up to that point of his own poetic credo, Prešeren wrote to Vraz on 5 July 1837:

The tendency of our [i.e., Prešeren's] songs and other literary activities is none other than to cultivate our mother tongue; if you people have another goal, then you will achieve it with difficulty. The unification of all Slavs in *one* literary language will probably remain a pious wish. It certainly will not be easy for you to raise the Styrian Croatian dialect onto the philological throne. At the same time even backward striving is better than apathy toward everything national.[74]

Gentle though these words were, they hit home. By the end of 1837 Vraz had definitely been lost to Slovene literature. Gaj was publishing his Štokavian poetry in his Zagreb newspaper the *Illyrian Morning Star*, Vraz abjured Slovene,[75] and a new phase of the Illyrian Movement began, one which aimed at the elimination of Slovene as a literary language and its replacement by Serbo-Croatian.[76]

Vraz maintained that the position of the Slovenes was hopeless. They were too few and too heavily infiltrated by Germans. There-

fore, he reasoned, it would be better for them to survive as Slavs,
even if that meant abandoning Slovene, than to be swallowed up as
Slovenes by the Austro-Germans.[77] Prešeren, though rejecting such
arguments—he wrote Vraz that he would rather be a swineherd
than king of the dead[78]—did not have the initiative to counteract
them. In the face of Illyrian attacks, strict censorship, and his own
depression, he retreated into almost total social passivity.

But the day after Vraz left Ljubljana for the second time, two
Polish exiles arrived. They had been expelled from their native
Galicia for seditious activities. In his very first letter to Vraz,
Prešeren mentioned the arrival of Emil Korytko and Bogusław
Horodyński, and that, as a result of his friendship with the former,
he had learned some Polish and even translated a poem by
Mickiewicz from Polish into German.[79] Korytko became more than
the poet's Polish teacher, however: with his youthful enthusiasm
and energy he enlivened the Carniolan intellectual scene. No sooner
had he settled in Ljubljana than he began planning to publish a
collection of Carniolan folk songs.[80] Thanks probably to Prešeren
and his two friends, Kastelic and Smolè, he became aware that the
Croatian Illyrian Movement was exerting great pressure on the
recently reborn Slovene revival. Therefore he undertook to reaffirm
a specifically Slovene ethnic identity by collecting Carniolan folk
songs. And, to steal some of the Illyrians' fire, he planned to publish
these not in the traditional "bohoričica" script, but in the new
"gajica"—so named in honor of Gaj—adapted where appropriate to
Slovene usage.

Korytko worked very fast. By his death in 1839, after he and
Prešeren had collected folk literature for only two years, he had
enough material to fill five volumes, which were published posthumously by his Carniolan friends as Slovene Songs of the Carniolan
People (1839-1844). For a variety of reasons the volumes were
printed in the traditional script, but Korytko's intentions alone were
sufficient to convince other Slovenes that some Illyrian proposals
might be adapted successfully to Slovene, without however compromising the position of the nation and its language. Thus Kastelic
and Smolè planned to publish the fifth number of the Bee in the
"gajica" (which actually happened, but not until 1848).[81]Plans were
also launched to print a Slovene newspaper in Ljubljana, to be
entitled, meaningfully enough, the Illyrian News, with a literary
supplement called the Illyrian Mercury.[82] Prešeren and his collaborators failed to bring this enterprise to fruition. But in 1843, another
publicist began to issue in Ljubljana the Peasants' and Artisans'

News. Some of its articles were printed in the "gajica" almost from
the beginning; by 1845 the paper was appearing completely in the
new orthography.

It was the issue of folk songs, however, not alphabets, which
crystallized the differences between Prešeren and Vraz. The poet's
two letters to him, of 19 July 1838 and 26 October 1840,[83] give clear
evidence of Prešeren's determination to resist Illyrianism in Slovenia. In the first he wrote:

Korytko is collecting our folk songs and information concerning the customs
and usages of our fatherland. He applied to Dr. Ljudevit Gaj in order to
have the folksongs printed with Czech Illyrian letters [i.e., "gajica"],
however he received a rather puzzling answer. It was indicated to him that
Dr. Gaj's office was prepared to undertake the printing only under the
condition that the songs exhibited a purely Illyrian, not *Carniolan* tendency,
which is almost incomprehensible to me, in that traditions of bygone times
in my opinion support no tendency of the present, also the language of
folksongs is not changeable without transforming its essence. It would
appear that Dr. Gaj and other Slavic literati are serious in the idea that
Slovene and the Illyrian Serbian language should be blended into one, or
even more, that Slovene as a written language must cease and henceforth
only Serbian be written. I am personally convinced of the unrealizability of
this idea. . . .

Even more explicit is the poet's rejection of Slovene in the heavily
ironic tone of the later letter:

By allowing our "dwarf literature" to slumber in those areas which do not
spring directly from folk life, we hope to earn thanks from you (majestic
plural). Should you be in touch with Kollár, Šafařík, etc., I ask you to
inform them of this good news. It would be wonderful if Slavdom in our
territories were to disappear, so that future specialists of the subject would
be spared the trouble of not only studying but even superficially regarding
a dialect which lacks many modern expressions, which, however, can give
clues to many now lost derivations and constructions.

Still, Prešeren concludes, as always, with a gentle reproach, couched
in humor: "In any event I wish not only Pan-Slavism, but even Pan-
Illyrianism the greatest success; I believe, however, that one should
leave everything which has sprouted up standing until Judgment
Day so that the Lord (το Παν) on the last day will be able to separate
the good from the evil. [Signed] . . . Your and Slavdom's true
friend. . . ."[84]

It was courageous of Prešeren to defend his "dwarf literature," which as Vraz pointed out, had no native heroes to depict nor native resources for the publication and sale of books.[85] But in point of fact Slovene was developing a hero, and it was Prešeren himself. In 1838 Franc Malavašič published the first article on Prešeren as the national poet of Slovenia.[86] Furthermore, Prešeren and Smolè were issuing the Slovene "classics" of the late eighteenth and early nineteenth centuries in new editions, as well as Smolè's own translations into Slovene of two popular English plays. Had not death intervened, first in carrying off Korytko, then, at the end of 1840, Smolè, it is possible that Prešeren and his circle would have gone even farther in laying the foundations of a Slovene literary culture of high quality as early as the 1840s.

As it was, the lead slipped from Prešeren's hands, to be taken up by those with an equal commitment to Slovene nationhood, but without Prešeren's taste or ability (especially the publisher of the *News*, Bleiweis; the poetaster who for a few decades outshone Prešeren, Jovan Vesel-Koseski; and Malavašič, who came to disdain Prešeren and support Koseski). Vraz, who visited Ljubljana in 1841 for the last time, must have had a sense of triumph.[87] Certainly circumstances seemed to show that he had acted correctly in abandoning Slovene. His poetry was being published in Zagreb by Gaj and could be read by all Croats and Serbs familiar with the "gajica." The Illyrian Movement was at its peak: when the Russian Slavist I. I. Sreznevsky visited Gaj in Zagreb in the spring of 1841, he was regaled with plans for an Illyrian cultural center, which was to include a theater, a museum, a "matica" (a national publishing house) a cultural society, and so on.[88] And Vraz's native Styria seemed to be moving closer to Zagreb and farther away from Ljubljana. The loss of Graz to the Illyrian side would surely have sounded the death knell for a viable Slovene culture. For Prešeren at least, 1841 marked the end of the battle. Thereafter, bedeviled by personal problems and crippled by the loss of all his friends and collaborators, he retreated from the intellectual and cultural scene. In one of his last letters to Vraz he wrote: "My name in the Slovene world may be presumed forgotten."[89] His high-mindedness seemed gone, and the poor sales of his collection of 1846 seemed only to confirm the fact that he had failed as a poet.

IV   *Prešeren's Legacy*

Modern Slovene literature suffers no lack of effulgent apprecia-tions of Prešeren's poetry and the role he played in creating the

Slovene nation.[90] But in the years after 1841 and indeed the decade and a half after the poet's death, Prešeren's greatness was not an accepted fact. The poet had been right to say his name had been extinguished among the Slovenes, at least for a time.

Prešeren was rescued from oblivion, however, by three "Young Slovenes," members of a group opposed to Bleiweis, Koseski, and the party known as "Old Slovenes."[91] Fran Levstik, Jožef Jurčič, and especially Josip Stritar in two moves reestablished Prešeren's reputation and destroyed Koseski's. In their criticism of the latter,[92] and in the republication of the former's *Poems* (in *Prešeren, . . . Kernels from the Home Field*, 1866), they exposed Koseski for the patriotic fraud he was. More important they initiated the cult of Prešeren. Stritar wrote the introduction to the volume. First, he outlined as best he could the facts of Prešeren's life. And he surveyed Prešeren's poetry, basing the poet's greatness squarely on the superiority of his verse. He ranked Prešeren as the foremost poetic genius of the Slovene people, on a par with Shakespeare for the English, Racine for the French, Goethe for the Germans, Pushkin for the Russians, Mickiewicz for the Poles, and Dante for the Italians.[93] Prešeren, he claimed, sprang from the almost barren field of Slovene poetry before him to sing of "love, patriotism, and longing after an ideal."[94] His poetry was at once personal, national, and universal. As lyricist, epic poet, and satirist, he blended his experiences with the poetry of other nations and eras to create a truly unique Slovene oeuvre. Stritar concluded his introduction with words which can still be cited today to describe Prešeren's importance to his people and to all who care for poetry:

Proudly we dare to say that our Prešeren too is one of those chosen instruments through whom heavenly beauty, celestial poetry are revealed on earth. When the nations are called before the seat of judgment to give an account of how they used their talents, to tell how they each took part in the universe of human culture, the small Slovene nation will dare to show itself without fear among the others carrying one slender book, which is entitled *Prešeren's Poetry*.[95]

Having looked at length at the poet's life with all its struggles, we too now turn our attention to the source of Prešeren's greatness, his poetry.

CHAPTER 5

Slovene Poems

IT IS difficult to know precisely what role poetry played in Prešeren's life. Witnesses tell us that from earliest childhood he composed little ditties and loved to rhyme.[1] From 1819 on we can be reasonably sure he was, if not creating poetry, then at least translating it. We have his poetic texts from 1825 or 1826, and a quasi-poetic text from 1824, the letter to his parents, which, as Boris Paternu points out, contains two fairly involved metaphors and must therefore be considered the beginning of his poetic career.[2] At critical moments in his mature years he sometimes turned to poetic creation: upon falling in love with Julija Primic, at the death of Matija Čop and Andrej Smolè, in his quarrels with Kopitar and others. But events, both good and bad, did not consistently prompt him to write: we may recall his unpoetic affair with Ana Jelovšek, or the death of their first child. In the final analysis poetry seems to have been an independent activity of the poet's mind. On many occasions it may have helped him to confront and resolve his personal crises, but in other cases the biographical connection of some of his works is tenuous. As T. S. Eliot has noted, "the more perfect the artist, the more completely separate in him will be the man who suffers and the mind which creates."[3] In analyzing Prešeren's poetry, we must always keep in mind the poet's potential for independent, non-biographical artistic expression.

For this reason, I have chosen to deal with Prešeren's poems not, as the best modern treatment has done,[4] in the order in which they were composed. Rather I have elected to examine them by genre. What is lost thus in appreciating Prešeren's *development* as a poet—an undeniable advantage of the diachronic approach—is recompensed, I hope, by a more concise understanding of his *achievement* as a poet. Consideration by genre enables us to concentrate on the poems' formal perfection, their strongest point, and to follow thereby the precedent established by Prešeren himself, for whom questions of structure seem to have outweighed every other consideration in the composition of his poetry.[5] We need only remember for confirmation of this point that the anthology of 1846, Prešeren's definitive arrangement of his poetry, was itself ordered by genre. Thus we proceed from the biographical data left us by the suffering poet, the first half of our monograph, to a closer examination of his creative mind, which comprises the second half.[6]

In the sections that follow, selected poems from each section of Prešeren's anthology are examined as representatives of their respective genres. Where artistic, thematic, or biographical considerations merit it, poems not included in the anthology are also treated here. Finally, Prešeren's German poems, which he was planning to publish in a companion volume to his Slovene work, are examined by genre in the following chapter.

I *Poems*

The slender volume entitled *Poems*, which Prešeren published on 15 December 1846, represents the poet's final efforts with his poetry. In writing out two separate complete manuscripts of the book for presentation to the censor, he altered both the style and substance of many of his earlier published poems. He arranged the texts he had decided to include—111 out of a total of 175 of his Slovene-language texts—by genre. And he prefaced the whole collection with a short poem entitled "Prosto srce" [The Free Heart, 1838]:[7]

> Sem dolgo upal in se bal,
> slovó sem upu, strahu dal;
> srcé je prazno, srečno ni,
> nazaj si up in strah želi.

> Long I hoped and long I feared,
> I said farewell to hope, to fear,
> My heart is empty, nor is it happy,
> It wants hope and fear to return.

This concise little poem offers us at the very beginning of *Poems* two valuable insights into the poet's thinking. First, it points out a fundamental flaw in the Creation, that is, that one can neither live with hope and fear, nor bear to live without them. The poet's fickle heart, first dismissing fear and hope, then wanting them back, is an analogue of the greater fickleness of the universe which allows such an impossible arrangement. Prešeren's poetry records above all else his dissatisfaction with such imperfections of life, as well as his attempts to come to terms with them. Second, "The Free Heart" clearly establishes as the center of the poet's concern his feeling, thinking self. The tribulations of his lyric "I" provide him with his richest, most poignant material. Many of the poems in the anthology and several not included there explore these two points which Prešeren's epilogue makes so economically at the outset.

II   Lyrics (Pesmi)

The pessimistic tone of the epigraph does not carry over immediately into the first section of the anthology, which contains nineteen "songs." This designation, technically imprecise, refers to the lyricism of the pieces contained therein.[8] Fittingly the first poem of the section is entitled "Strunam" [To My Lyre, 1831; literally "To the Strings"] and the last "Pevcu" [To the Singer, 1838].

"To My Lyre" commissions the anthology, as it were. The poet instructs his strings and his song to soften his hardhearted mistress. He is languishing without her and, even more important, his lyre may go silent if she does not relent. The function of his songs, then, is to melt his beloved's heart and ease his pain.

In this poem (trochaic tetrameter set in six quatrains with alternating masculine and feminine rhymes) Prešeren establishes at the outset the clear connection between the amorous and the poetic. Poetry is an instrument for the winning of love; love, especially unrequited, is, on the other hand, the inspiration of poetry. He is the troubadour trying to woo an aloof lady. But his Petrarchan pose belies the very serious note he strikes at the end of the fifth stanza: "If she does not soon grow gracious, / You [i.e., the strings] may grow silent forever." Death, too, enters the equation of love and poetry, for the silencing of the strings means the end of the poetry and the death of the poet. Love, death, and poetry, all introduced in this first poem, form a thematic nexus which recurs often throughout Prešeren's work.

"Kam?" (Where To? 1835; German "Wohin?"), a crisp, brief lyric of six two-line stanzas of iambic tetrameter, presents the poet in another of his favorite poses: the restless, distraught, suicidal lover. Like the clouds of the sky or waves of the sea when tossed by a storm, he is driven aimlessly by his despair across the face of the earth. Surcease of sorrow will not be his "above the earth." He is unloved: death, perhaps by suicide, ever an option in Prešeren's philosophy,[9] may provide the only resolution to his torment.

The poem's imagery, as is evident from even this short summary, is unexciting. Here as elsewhere the poet hewed far closer to the stylize conventions of Renaissance love lyrics than to the innovative, colorful, dynamic tropes of his contemporaries, the romantics. Wherein, then, lies the appeal of Prešeren's poetry? Precisely in those features which escape translation: the sound of the Slovene verse; the purity, simplicity, and elegance of the vocabulary; and the delicate but driving rhythm of the poem. The problem with Prešeren is also his greatest achievement, and "Where To?" typifies both to some degree: he is at once the champion and victim of his language. The poem demonstrates the suppleness of Prešeren's Slovene, yet only those relatively few people who can read it in the original will ever have a sense of what that means.

The following five poems, among the last love lyrics Prešeren wrote although they are placed here at the beginning of the anthology, continue to offer conventional imagery phrased in the poet's unique Slovene. Thematically they catalog the poet's final disenchantment with love (what Paternu calls his "demythologizing" of love)[10] as the ruling passion of his life. "Ukazi" [Orders, 1842] tells how the poet's beloved has commanded him to leave off his pursuit of her. In all he is obedient, except at the command to forget her, which he cannot do "until this heart stops beating in my breast." "K slovesu" [In Farewell, 1842] reveals the poet's willingness to end the futile game of one-sided love. He is ready to bid his love goodbye and return to his old mistress, Patience. She will help him withstand life's burden until his last mistress, "White Death," conquers all his misfortunes. Both these poems, so similar in theme, are identical in structure: trochaic tetrameter, six quatrains.

"Sila spomina" [The Power of Memory, 1844], on the other hand, makes use of a ternary meter (seven quatrains of dactylic hexameter), a rare phenomenon in Prešeren's poetry—it figures in only fourteen percent of his verse in the anthology.[11] The tone of this poem is distinct as well: for a change, the poet assumes the upper hand by assuring his mistress she is condemned to remember him and his poetry until her dying day. He stands proudly by, as indifferent to her plight as she earlier had been unmoved by his.[12]

The poem "Zgubljena vera" [Lost Faith, 1842][13] reveals even more clearly the poet's disenchantment with his mistress and with love in general. For though she continues to be beautiful, the loved one has forfeited his affectionate faith in her by "one single glance." Trust is gone:

> En sam pogled je vzel jo preč,
> nazaj ne bo je níkdar več.
> Ak bi živela vékomej,
> kar si mi b'la, ne boš naprej.
> Srcé je moje bilo *oltar*,
> préd *bogstvo* ti, zdaj—lepa *stvar*.

> One single glance has taken it off,
> Never more will it return.
> Wert thou to live forever more,
> What once wert, shalst ne'er be again.
> My heart was once an *altar*,
> Before thou wert its *godhead*, now—a pretty *thing*.

The two-line stanzas of iambic tetrameter sound harsh in this poem, probably because of the uniform masculine rhymes in each of the eleven stanzas.

The concluding poem in this group of five is "Mornar" [The Sailor, 1843].[14] Each of its seven stanzas is composed of two tercets: two iambic tetrameters and a trimeter, with a rhyme scheme *a a b c c b*. Here the poet bids his faithless mistress farewell forever. He wishes her happiness on land, as he returns to the sea to seek his "hope." His faithfulness, which has been tested in many a foreign port, obviously meant nothing to her, as did her promise to him to remain true. Now the sailor knows to trust only the sea, which alone will help him overcome his painful memories. At least on the surface "The Sailor" seems to be a statement of complete resignation. The poet has decided love on earth is impossible, and he is now resigned to pursuing some other kind of satisfaction on the sea: "My hope has gone to sea, / Let's try to sail after it!" But resignation implies a willingness to harden one's heart to what was once loved. While that clearly is the case in "Lost Faith," where the beloved becomes "a pretty thing," the process of hardening in "The Sailor" is moot: "Memory passes on the deep, / Each day revives again / Love's agonies!" Not even the sea can end the agony brought on by each new day. Only the end of new days, death, can do that, as Prešeren's German translation of the foregoing tercet makes clear: "He who is dead has found rest, / Love's wounds are torn anew / At each morning light." Thus resignation is not the theme here, but death. The sea is a metaphor for death, hardly an uncommon transformation in romantic poetry, and the sailor's "return to the sea" is in fact the poet's longing for death. The "demythologization" of the poet's love did not result in his being able to live: on the contrary, by doing away with his unreciprocated, intense love for his mistress, the poet did away with his reason for living. Once again the only suitable antonym for love, at least in poetry, is death.

A tone of mirth and merriment is sounded, quite by contrast, in the lyric entitled "Zdravljica" [The Toast, 1844], a drinking song. But the tone and shape—the poem is a "carmen figuratum," or "picture poem," which depicts a wine glass[15]—are deceptive, for despite the froth the poem has much substance. Edvard Kardelj has cited it as a seminal statement on Slovene patriotism.[16] And Anton Slodnjak has pointed out the polemic nature of "The Toast," in contrasting it with Jovan Vesel-Koseski's patriotic, Austro-Slavist paean to the Hapsburg emperor, "Slovenia to Kaiser Ferdinand" (1843).[17] Coming as it does from the end of Prešeren's writing career, it would seem to represent his definitive statement about love of country. It was intended for publication in *Poems*, but because the censor objected to one line of it, Prešeren removed the entire piece from the anthology. It came to light only in 1848 in volume 5 of the *Carniolan Bee*.

Though it never actually names the country, "The Toast" celebrates Slovenia in no uncertain terms. Each of the eight stanzas glorifies one of the nation's attributes: wine, the land, the freedom to come, the future independence of all Slavs, Slovene women, Slovene youth, all neighbors also suffering in tyranny, the poet's good friends and fellow drinkers. Even if Prešeren can scarcely be considered a revolutionary, his understanding of the destiny of his nation definitely stood to the left of the popular view of the day, represented by Koseski and Bleiweis. In Prešeren's poetry there is no trace of affection for the incorporation of Slovenia within Austria nor for the Hapsburg dynasty. On the other hand there is a clear sense of a "greater Slovenia," a union of all Slovene speakers scattered through six provinces of the Austrian empire. Whether this unification was meant to be political or something else is difficult to say. Prešeren never used the term "Slovenia" itself in his poetry, employing instead "slovenstvo," "the body of Slovene speakers," and various circumlocutions, such as "the Slovene world," "the home of the Slovenes," and others.[18] But the first and greatest of all Slovene poets perceived clearly the necessity for Slovenes to be united. Of the benefits of such a union he sings in "The Toast."

Perhaps the most outstanding feature of the poet's ethnic consciousness is its very lack of exclusive ethnocentricity. Given the

precarious state of the Slovene group on the border of the Slavic
and Germanic worlds, Prešeren might have called for consolidation
and isolation, to preserve what was "purely" Slovene, as did for
example Kopitar. But to his credit he realized that the destiny of the
nation lay in the larger context of the Slavic world and even beyond
that, in all of humanity. In the stanza whose first line caused the
poem to be dropped from the anthology he writes of the Slavs (here
in the translation of Janko Lavrin):[19]

> Edinost, sreča, sprava
> k nam nazaj se vrnejo;
> otrok, kar ima slava,
> vsi naj si v róke sežejo,
> de oblast
> in z njo čast,
> ko préd, spet naša boste last!

> Let peace, glad conciliation,
> Come back to us throughout the land!
> Toward their destination
> Let Slavs henceforth go hand in hand!
> Thus again
> Will honor reign
> To justice pledged in our domain.

And of the whole world he says:[20]

> Živé naj vsi naródi,
> ki hrepené dočakat' dan,
> ko, koder sonce hodi,
> prepir iz svéta bo pregnan,
> ko rojak
> prost bo vsak,
> ne vrag, le sosed bo mejak!

> God's blessings on all nations,
> Who long and work for that bright day,
> When o'er earth's habitations
> No war, no strife shall hold its sway;
> Who long to see
> That all men free
> No more shall foes, but neighbors be.

Prešeren's view of Slovenes living in harmony includes of necessity peace in the entire world. This idea, articulated here at the beginning of the Slovene revival, has contributed much to the peculiar quality of Slovene patriotism, which, in Eastern Europe, resembles most closely that of the Czechs for its sensitivity to foreign events and sense of patient accommodation.[21] The role of "The Toast" in formulating the national ideal cannot be overstated. And as the first major statement on the national theme in *Poems*, it sets the tone for the development of the topic that occurs in later sections.

The last three poems before the coda to the lyric section differ in style, but all three treat the same theme, infidelity. "Od železne ceste" [About the Railway, 1845], the first of Prešeren's poems to appear in the *Peasants' and Artisans' News* in the new script, "gajica," deals with mutual planned infidelity, in effect mock adulterousness, on the part of a simple (peasant?) boy and girl who are anticipating the coming of the railway line to Ljubljana. The poem, eighteen quatrains long, in trochaic tetrameter, is arranged in the form of a dialogue between the boy and the girl. It ends with a marriage proposal and a simple aphorism ("A husband always dissipates least / When he travels with his wife"). On the whole one is reminded of Prešeren's letter to Stanko Vraz (12 December 1843), where he writes: "Presently I am working on Carniolan songs which should please the peasant boys; when I have composed a few, I will publish my carmina [i.e., his anthology]."[22]

"Zapušena" [The Abandoned Girl, 1835] is an early poem treating infidelity from the point of view, untypically, of the jilted girl. She forgives her lover everything, blesses him and his new mistress, and prays for death to visit her before the two wed. Usually in Prešeren unfaithfulness is characteristic of the beautiful, proud woman. But here and in "About the Railway," infidelity characterizes the male as well, and with equally devastating results for the abandoned partner. She has one source of consolation, however, that is denied to the male, and of that the poet sings in the following poem.

"Nezakonska mati" [The Unwed Mother, 1845], a brief lyric the poet may have composed for Ana Jelovšek, the "unwed mother" of his three illegitimate children, tells of the consolation the abandoned lover finds in her bastard child. Though she too suffers the pains of abandonment—public and private shame, emotional agony—she still has something to love, thereby overcoming the worst consequence of her partner's infidelity, which is the deprivation of the love object. In other Prešeren poems on this theme, loss of love is total, and the only alternative available to the abandoned lover is death. Here one kind of love has been successfully, if painfully, replaced by another, resulting in life and the continued will to live it:

> On, ki ptíce pod nebam živi,
> nàj ti dá srečne, veséle dni!
> Al te je tréba biló, al ne,
> védno bom sŕčno ljubíla te!

> May he who gives life to the fowls of the air
> Grant you happy, joyous days!
> Whether you were needed or not,
> I shall always love you with all my heart!

"The Unwed Mother" appears at first blush also to be folk in origin. Certainly the diction of the poem is simple. But its structural intricacy belies its folk tone. Irregularities of the meter and rhyme, repetition of verses, paralleling of stanzas, the reference to Matthew 6:26 in the last strophe, all point to a sophisticated poetic sensibility, not folk art. The poem's cohesiveness metrically and poetically bespeaks the tranquillity of its speaker. No anxiety mars the mother's monologue with her infant; she answers all her questions herself, she has peace. Prešeren's genius is displayed in this poem perhaps more clearly than in any other of his shorter works. He who in his own life was incapable of peace in his erotic affairs was as a poet nonetheless capable of depicting the most heartfelt tranquillity. The early Prešeren enthusiast, Fran Levstik, also appreciated this poem's artistry, so much so that he called "The Unwed Mother" the best of Prešeren's works.[23] While this estimate, in the light of the poet's sonnets and his epic, seems exaggerated, still among the lyrics the poem may rank as the most outstanding.

The placement of the last poem in the lyric section, "Pevcu" [To the Singer, 1838; also translatable as "To the Poet"], is quite deliberate, for it counterbalances "To My Lyre" at the beginning. As all the critics agree, it is one of the most revealing statements on art in Prešeren's canon. Moreover, it dates from a critical period in his poetic life, just after which, as Anton Slodnjak says, "the metric-rhythmic structure of his poems began to loosen."[24]

The structure of "To the Singer" is quite remarkable. There are five stanzas, each with an assonant rhyme in a different vowel (*á, é, í, ó, ú*). The first and last stanzas are two lines long, the second and fourth are three, and the middle is four. Each first line is a single iambic foot.[25] The meter of the remaining lines of each stanza is amphibrachic tetrameter, with irregularities. Each stanza is one complete sentence, the first four being rhetorical questions, and the fifth a double imperative; each stanza is punctuated with an exclamation point.

In effect, "To the Singer" defines the role of the poet: it is he who "knows how to brighten the dark night that bruises the soul; to drive off the bird of prey that claws at the heart all day; who revives the memory of the past, conceals the hopelessness of the future, and avoids the emptiness of the present." How can you be a poet, he asks, unless you can bear both heaven and hell in one and the same breast? "Of your state / Be mindful, bear it without peace!"

The real poet, then, assumes a sacrificial role in his society. In order to bring enlightenment and tranquillity to others, he offers up his own peace of mind. Poetry becomes a sacred obligation which, however, can destroy the poet. Yet the poet has no choice but to accept his role and endure its tensions. What tensions those are the poet has already made clear in "The Free Heart," which was also written in 1838. Both poems affirm that poetry is the product of a poet's suffering mind, the result of the unresolved, unresolvable tensions of his life.

Ironically, however, at the very moment the poet was citing his own psychic pain as the source of his art, a reduction of those tensions seems to have taken place in his life. We have not only the facts of his biography to substantiate this—the demise of his hopes for Julija, the beginning of his relationship with Ana—but Slodnjak's pertinent observation as well, that his later poetry lacked a certain dynamic tension, and the fact that in 1839 he wrote no verse at all. Hope and fear, once his chief inspiration, were no longer to be found in his now more relaxed heart, and his poetic practice suffered as a result. But how then are we to take "To the Singer"? Was it Prešeren's "swan song," the valedictory to his life as a poet?

Prešeren's little poem on poets captures perfectly the utter isolation to which society had consigned his creative genius in the late 1830s. As a man he may not have been alone, but as a sophisticated poet of great refinement and keen insight he had no one to turn to. Cut off from the world, sensing perhaps the loss of the inner tension which had allowed him to create his finest poetry, the poet desperately needed encouragement, but the world remained unresponsive. In "To the Poet" therefore he addressed the only person who could give him that encouragement: himself. And he did so precisely as "the genius who creates" speaking to "the man who suffers," to convince himself to persevere, to avoid the lure of suicide, for the sake of his higher calling, poetry. "To the Singer" is in the final analysis Prešeren's most intimate, most revealing poem. And it is a fitting cap to his section of lyric verse.

Of the ten poems we might consider lyric but which were not included in Prešeren's anthology,[26] only two were published in the poet's lifetime. The others remained in manuscript until discovered by one or another of his posthumous editors. He may very well have forgotten that he had composed these poems—most are very early efforts, some without particular artistic merit. Or he may have suppressed some of them for political reasons. Whatever the case, two are worth our close interest here.

Obviously political and significant poetically is "Elegija svojim rojakam" [Elegy to One's Fellow Countrymen, 1832]. Like "The Toast," "Elegy" sings of the beauty of the Slovene homeland, epitomized for the poet by Carniola. The land is their mother, Carniolans are all brothers: what is lacking, however, is any love for the "mother" by her "sons." The poet excoriates the acquisitive drives of his countrymen, their slavishness before all foreign things, their indifference to their own traditions and their own poets. While "Elegy" lacks the splendid pan-humanism of "The Toast," it does introduce a vital theme of Prešeren's patriotic verse, that of "Orpheism," or the suffering poet as spokesman and conscience of his nation. Slavic poets in particular were keenly aware of their role as the tongue of the nation: it came naturally to them to speak for peoples who, in the eyes of the West, from which the romantic impulses radiated, had remained mute for so long. "Elegy" is Prešeren's earliest contribution to this trend; it is a precursor of his greatest elaboration of the theme in "A Wreath of Sonnets."

The other item worthy of attention in this group of uncollected lyrics belongs only tentatively to Prešeren's pen. It was recorded, so the story goes, from the spoken words of the poet by Miha Kastelic, the editor of the *Carniolan Bee*. Despite the obscurity of its origin, however, every modern scholar accepts it as Prešeren's own and, indeed, usually ascribes much importance to it. The quatrain is based on Heraclitus' famous dictum that "panta rhei" ("all things flow"):

Kar je, beži;
al beg ni Bog?
ki vodi vekomaj v ne-bó,
kar je, kar b'lo je, in kar bo.

What is, flows;
Is the flow not God?
That leads always to nonbeing/heaven
What is, what was, and what will be.[27]

The "point" lies in the Slovene pun which equates "ne-bó" ("nonbeing") with "nebó" ("heaven"). Thus God can be construed as leading all things to heaven, while "the flow" leads all things to nothingness.

The ambiguity of this verse underlines an ambivalence in the poet's theology. In terms of faith and practice, Prešeren was a lapsed Catholic from 1824 until he lay on his deathbed in 1849,[28] thus during his entire poetic period. Like his friend Čop he was indifferent to matters of public religion. In 1832, for example, the two friends traveled to Vrba, still the home of the Prešeren family, to attend the festivities surrounding the first mass celebrated by the poet's brother Jurij, but not to attend the mass itself. Despite his mother's wishes, Prešeren firmly rejected a clerical career for himself;[29] and in the 1830s he evinced a great interest in the German movement, an offshoot of Hegelianism, which sought to "demythologize" the life of Christ and retell it in human, not divine terms.[30] In essence he was, as Kos says, areligious,[31] without the firm convictions about God of either an atheist or a believer. His philosophy was anthropocentric, while his understanding of the organization of the universe tended more to the fatalistic than the Christian.

Yet for all of his presumed indifference, Prešeren did die reconciled to the church and its faith. Nor was this final act of contrition completely out of keeping with his earlier life. Much of Prešeren's poetry makes liberal use of religious, particularly Christian symbols, motifs, and ideas. He himself said he was both "faithless and yet faithful."[32] By all accounts he respected the Catholic faith of his parents.[33] In the final analysis, we might perhaps assume that, since he nowhere abjures faith in a personal God, he held some belief in one, although for one reason or another he was unwilling or unable to articulate His attributes.

Consequently "indifference" may be the wrong word to apply to the poet's religious sentiments. Judging by all he wrote, and particularly by "What is, Flows," whose whole point is based on ambivalence, not indifference, toward God, Prešeren exhibited not rejection, but hesitancy. God and His part in human affairs were a mystery which the poet, like many of his fellow romantics, could not or would not apprehend. But if his poetry does not seem to us today religious in the conventional sense of the word, nonetheless we would be mistaken to dismiss from the poet's corpus of themes all religious considerations. For they are important to a poem like "What is, Flows," which we might view after all as an attempt to name God, and vital to other poems where faith, life, death, and life's meaning are treated as elements of a universe which the poet does not want to believe is completely absurd.

III *Ballads and Romances*

From the very personal pieces in the lyrical section of *Poems*, with their varying forms and wide range of themes, we move now to "Ballads and Romances," far less intimate genres which include some of Prešeren's earliest poetry. The first four works, "Hčere svet" [The Daughter's Advice, 1828], "Učenec" [The Student, 1829], "Dohtar" [The Doctor, 1829], and "Turjaška Rozamunda" [Rozamunda of Turjak, 1831], are romances in the strict sense, a special type of ballad distinguished by its structure: octosyllabic lines whose even-numbered verses end in a vowel rhyme (i.e., assonance), while odd-numbered verses are unrhymed.[34] As with the ballad in general these four romances concentrate on a single episode, heighten the drama through the description of intense, immediate action and dialogue, and avoid any personal assertions on the part of the poet, who stands apart from his work.[35] Until Prešeren the romance was unknown in Slovene. But probably at the urging of Čop, he introduced it as part of his program of bringing into Slovene literature the poetic forms used successfully by other European nations.

As both verse experiment and poetry with enduring aesthetic qualities, Prešeren's romances must be considered a major achievement. Without any Slovene precursors he composed crisp, colorful verse. The drive of the lines never fails; however often these poems are read, they continue to be engaging. The anecdotes or tales they tell do not become tiresome, simple as they sometimes are, because their racy language and subtle assonances, far more than the plot, still pique our sensibilities today.

Much the same can be said about the following three poems. As ballads and not specifically romances their structure is somewhat looser. On the other hand, their plots are more sophisticated. "Judovsko dekle" [The Jewish Girl, 1845], octosyllabic with, however, not one but a variety of assonances in its stanzas, stands in counterpoint to "Rozamunda of Turjak," which precedes it. (Prešeren's placement of the poems in the anthology frequently provides insight into his understanding of them.) This very late poem depicts a gentile suitor who is powerless to overcome the obstacles in the path of his love because his beloved is Jewish. When faced with the same problem, the knightly hero of "Rozamunda" abducted his Moslem ladylove, had her converted, then wed her. But that poem dates from a period in Prešeren's life when the poet himself was more sanguine about his own possibilities for happiness in love, whatever the circumstances. The lesson of "The Jewish Girl" seems to be that even the strongest affections eventually fall victim to factors beyond the control of an ardent lover.

The following poem is entitled, meaningfully, "Zdravilo ljubezni" [The Cure for Love, 1837]. Its decasyllabic lines, rhyming couplets, repeated verses, and structure (a series of three incidents leading to a resolution) suggest a folk song. It is clearly intended as a response to the preceding poem, for the "cure for love," typically Prešernian, is death. So too in the next one, "Lenora" [Lenore, 1824?], which is Prešeren's very early and extraordinarily successful translation of Gottfried August Bürger's ballad of the same name, composed in 1774: the heroine, uncontrollably in love with her William, who has been lost at war, summons him through her frantic prayers to come back to her. When he does arrive to take her away, she realizes only too late that he is dead; undaunted, however, she returns with him to the grave. Lenore's excessive faithfulness to her "demon lover" no doubt appealed to and repelled the poet at the same time. On the one hand, he too longed for a mistress as faithful as Lenore, but on the other the price he would have to pay for such unrelenting devotion was high. Prešeren's handling of the ottava rima of the original is masterful: nothing of Lenore's passion, the wild ride on her lover's horse, nor her fearful death is lost in the Slovene version of the poem.

Also dating from the same period and having a similar plot is the ballad "Povodni mož" [The Water Sprite, 1824?]. Based on a legend from Slovene history, this poem remains perhaps one of the most popular of Prešeren's works. Its amphibrachic Alexandrines are read

today for much the same reason they were read with such enthusiasm when they appeared in the first *Carniolan Bee* in 1830: they
combine every poetic feature of the Slovene language—rhyme,
assonance, alliteration, free-word order, elipsis, inflectional richness
and expressiveness, flexible stress—into a concise rendering of a
Slovene legend for the sole purpose of providing aesthetic enjoyment to a Slovene audience. Prešeren's tale of proud Uršika, who
flirts with the men of Ljubljana until she meets her match in the
"water sprite," another "demon lover," who carries her off into the
waves of the Ljubljanica River in a dance every bit as wild as
Lenore's ride, proved the artistic possibilities of Slovene. "The
Water Sprite" says something in Slovene which could not be as well
said in any other language, not because in some linguistic way
Slovene is superior to others, but because a genial poet saw how to
make the most of the linguistic possibilities Slovene offers in order
to compose an enjoyable, readable, compelling—in short an aesthetic—text.

The remaining five ballads of this section are among the most
important poetry Prešeren wrote, for in the traditional biographical
view, they reveal much about Prešeren's own sufferings in the latter
half of the 1830s and the beginning of the 1840s. In them the poet
expressed most clearly his feelings on all the major themes of his
life: poetry, love, life.[36]

Prešeren composed the first of them, "Prekop" [Reburial, 1835],
along with a German translation, "Die Wiederbestattung") immediately after the tragic death of Matija Čop. Already in a state of
depression verging on the suicidal due to Julija Primic's indifference
to him,[37] the poet was brought to the brink of self-destruction by
the loss of his closest friend. Indeed, he may have even attempted
suicide.[38] Suicide is the subject of "Reburial."

A young poet, "not rich or well-known," takes poison because his
beloved, Severa, does not respond to his poems. His body is soon
discovered, but, since no one suspects he killed himself, he is buried
in hallowed ground, according to the regular rites of the church.
The priest performing the service hastens it, however, for he must
conduct a marriage immediately after: Severa's. That night, as he
returns to the church from the wedding festivities, the priest hears a
loud row from the cemetery. There he finds the poet quarreling
with the other corpses. The poet explains to the priest that he
cannot rest in hallowed ground because he killed himself, "so not to
be in my lover's way." The next morning the priest has him reburied
with the thieves.

The autobiographical elements of the poem seem obvious. Furthermore, the formal precision of the poem is quite extraordinary: it is one of only two of Prešeren's works to be composed in Nibelungen stanzas, a highly regarded epic verse form of German medieval literature.[39] Janko Kos suggests the epic form may have helped the poet distance himself from his poem, preserving an objectivity that lyric verse could not have sustained.[40] And the very controlled pattern of the meter and rhyme, perceives Juraj Martinović, counterbalances the lack of control and growing disharmony of the poet's emotional world.[41] "Reburial" then is a tautly expressed reflection on suicide, with, however, an antisuicidal moral. For even in death the poet can find neither rest nor honor.

Ten years later Prešeren again turned to the Nibelungen stanza. In "Neiztrohnjeno srce" [The Uncorrupted Heart, 1845] gravediggers come unexpectedly upon the body of a fair young man. They can hardly believe their eyes at the body's lack of corruption, but are even more astounded when the first puff of wind disintegrates the body but leaves the still beating heart intact. They learn from the gravestone that this is Dobroslav, a poet who would no longer compose after his beloved married another. Eventually he died, having maintained his silence to the end. Then an old man among the gravediggers affirms that before them is a poet's heart which cannot see corruption because of the poems still closed inside it. He tells them to leave it exposed to the sun and the moon, the breezes and the dew, to all the things that had inspired it in life, and then to reinter it. The next morning they return to find, however, that the poet's heart has melted in the early sunshine, "like the white snow of spring, so that there is nothing left to bury."

"The Uncorrupted Heart" was, with Čop's elegy, Prešeren's last major poem, and, although written a decade after "Reburial," it parallels the early poem closely. There is an exact equivalence of characters and setting between the two: the suicidal poet—Dobroslav; Severa—the beloved; the good people who find the body—the gravediggers; the priest—the old man; all in a cemetery, at a gravesite. But the most important parallel between the two poems lies in their moral. In "The Uncorrupted Heart" once again Prešeren depicts no rest for the poet even in death. Neither suicide nor a natural death are really the answer to his erotic failures. Death does not solve the problem of unrequited love, it merely begs the question forever. But if love cannot be responded to in its own terms, and if it cannot be killed off, how does the poet resolve the tension of his unfulfillment? In the poem the old man exposes the heart to the elements that inspired it once, to release the songs locked inside it. The metaphor is clear: only poetry can provide a rationale sufficient to permit a poet to continue facing an unhappy life.

The following ballad, "Ribič" [The Fisherman, 1838] is perhaps the most explicitly erotic poem Prešeren ever wrote, though by modern standards it seems quite restrained. A young fisherman, who feels a "pure" love for a star (the word "pure" is used twice), is guided over hazardous waters for many years by the light of that star. All is well until several mermaids appear, "naked to the waist" and pose the fisherman "provocative" questions: why does he wait so long for his star; why does he avoid them; why does his star stand so close to the hunter (i.e., the constellation)? Filled with despair as he realizes the truth implied in their questions, he heads out to sea, no longer following his guiding star. Is he chasing the mermaids, the poet asks, or running away from himself? In any event, the poet advises him who loves without hope not to follow the example of the fisherman, who in all probability was drowned.

While a certain autobiographical element doubtless inheres in this poem too—as one critic reminds us, Prešeren's clan name was Ribič[42]—"Ribič" is far more important as a statement on love than as biographic material. For in this poem the course of love is exposed: innocent love, for as long as it may exist, always remains unrequited; erotic love is more often than not fatal. Only one state is possible for him who would love faithfully and yet without hope of recompense: resignation.[43] Or so at least Prešeren would seem to have thought in 1838. We have only to recall the lyric "The Sailor" of 1843 to realize, however, that resignation was only the poet's temporary stance. Later the answer to the question of faithfulness in love would be found solely in death.

Of course in real life Prešeren did not resign himself to celibate faithfulness to his "star," Julija. Shortly before he wrote "The Fisherman" he had initiated his affair with Ana Jelovšek. In effect, like the fisherman, he had sailed off after an accessible, if less than heavenly mermaid. But the point of the poem lies in its depiction not of the real but of the ideal. And while it is always of interest to Prešeren's biographers to note the disharmony between the ideal the poet presented in his poems and the compromising reality of his life, to the critic the poem remains paramount. "The Fisherman" is Prešeren's first and most explicit statement that happiness cannot be found in love.

As "Reburial" and "The Uncorrupted Heart" stand together, so too do "The Fisherman" and the following ballad, "Ženska zvestoba" [Woman's Faithfulness, 1837]. It tells the tale of a young fiddler, a happy and handsome fellow who, each time he falls in love faithfully, is betrayed by his beloved, who runs off with another man. After each disappointment his instrument snaps a string, which he vows never to replace. Finally, left with only one string, he gives up women instead of risking the ruin of his fiddle. Learning to play on one string, "like Paganini," he sings forever after of woman's faithlessness, how it "trains the hand and clears the mind."

In effect the fiddler is finally faced with a choice between love and his art. Although each time he learns to play as well with one less string, nonetheless there comes a point when he will no longer be able to play at all unless he abandons his erotic pursuits. Unlike any other of Prešeren's statements on the theme of love, in this one the hero ends up happy for his renunciation with, moreover, an increased talent (necessary to play on ever fewer strings) *and* a good subject to sing about, his former loves. The newly chaste fiddler has become the greater artist for resigning himself to a life free of women's faithlessness and, by extension, women.

As if to confirm the artist's ideal commitment to celibacy—which, it must be repeated, Prešeren did not follow in his own life—the next poem speaks of a holy hermit who lives in the desert, singing God's praises and teaching the birds to do likewise. "Orglar" [The Minstrel, 1845] is the last and perhaps most significant poem of the ballad and romance section. As a statement on poetry it parallels "To the Singer," which concludes the lyric section. And as a statement on the ideal, it wraps up the preceding four ballads in a pointed, dramatic fashion.

The hermit teaches all the birds of the forest to sing to the Almighty except the nightingale which, try though the hermit might, still continues to sing "sweet melodies of his love." Eventually the holy man complains to God Himself that the nightingale will sing only his own, "not better" songs. To our surprise, however, God reprimands the hermit, not the bird:

> Pusti péti moj'ga slavca,
> kakor sem mu grlo stváril.
> Pel je v sužnosti železni
> Jeremíj žalòst globoko;
> pesem svojo je visoko

Salomon pel od ljubezni.
Kómur pevski duh sem vdihnil,
ž njim sem dal mu pesmi svoje;
drugih ne, le té naj poje,
dòkler, de bo v gróbu vtihnil.

The nightingale is just and right,
For what he sings is my command.
Once Jeremiah poured the wrongs
And griefs of bondage into rhyme,
King Solomon voiced for all time
His love in noble song of songs.
To him that I inspired I gave
The gift of melody divine;
So let him sing those songs of mine
Till he be silenced in the grave.[44]

Taken out of context of the preceding ballads, "The Minstrel" is
a beautiful plea for the poet whose subject is love. Given the fierce
resistance of the religious censorship to anything smacking of
eroticism, one can appreciate Prešeren's couching his petition in
terms of the God-ordained necessity that each poet create as he has
been given the talent to do. The religious imagery completely
dominates the poem, not only in direct mentionings—God, St.
Augustine, Jeremiah, Solomon—but in the overall structure as well.
The minstrel reminds us of Francis of Assisi, the poet-hermit who
loved the animals; and God's reprimanding the pious man in his
zeal has a New Testament ring about it. Whatever Prešeren's
religious status at the time, "The Minstrel" shows him to be
thoroughly imbued not only with Christian symbols, but with a
Christian ethic as well, that the poet is divinely obligated to use
honestly those gifts that have been given to him.

Within the context of the preceding poems, however, the meaning
of "The Minstrel" is further enriched. We have already noted the
connection between the chaste fiddler and the ascetic minstrel. The
latter is simply the further development of the former, and as such
represents "the poet" too, moreover a poet who has achieved a
higher understanding of his craft. Yet this same poet is reproved by
God, for the sake of the type of "poet" (the nightingale) who sings
monotonously on the one subject of love. The point, it seems to me,
is the following: "The Minstrel" is a plea not only for freedom from
external constraints on the poet's talent, but for an internal freedom
as well. The hermit must not repress the nightingale's natural song,

for it too is divine. Neither should the poet repress his natural inclination to sing of love, for the origins of his impulse to sing are wholly beyond him. Whatever the discomfort this erotic song may have for the poet who has achieved a greater awareness of love's sorrow and destructiveness, nonetheless the compensation for the current pain lies in the peace the unrepressed spirit eventually finds in the grave. The point of "Reburial" and "The Uncorrupted Heart" finds a counterpoint here in "The Minstrel": the only release the poet's spirit can find in this life is in his poetry; even a heightened consciousness of the absurdity of his feelings must never stand in the way of his poetic expression of them. Otherwise he will never be at peace with himself.[45]

IV *Various Poems*

Under the heading "Various Poems" Prešeren grouped twenty-nine quite disparate pieces. The six long poems which open the section are among his most complex statements on love and poetry. With one exception they date from the earliest years of his poetic career. Their appearance in the *Carniolan Bee* (1830-1834) had heralded a modern, secular, sophisticated literature written in Slovene. As one critic put it, after the publication of these first poems it had become impossible for other poets of conscience to compose banal verses in Slovene ever again.[46]

The form of these six longer poems is as varied as their content. Neither ballads nor sonnets, epics nor lyrical "songs," they are gathered together in this section precisely because they are structurally unique. In other sections, of course, genre was the organizing principle. Here, where generic considerations play no role, tone and attitude unify the section as a whole, for the "various poems" are written from the point of view of the poet in either a reflective or a polemical mood. Particularly the reflective poems, where the poet stands detached from the world and saddened by it, have become the crown and glory of Prešeren's entire opus.

The opening poem is "Zvezdogledam" [To Stargazers, 1826?], also known as "The False Practitioners" and "To Astrologers." With "Lenore" and "The Water Sprite" it was one of only three poems Prešeren decided to save when he burned the collection of his earliest verse.[47] He admitted that he had not "spared the file on them" in trying to improve them, but "as far as rhyme and meter are concerned, they bear evidence of when they were born."[48] "To Stargazers," composed of thirty-five lines of iambic trimeter, with

feminine endings but no rhyme, is perhaps the least successful of
the three thus held back from the flames. The poem's unity is
achieved by a structural device, the repetition of certain verses; and
by the conceit, which runs as follows: how can you astrologers
presume to read portents in all the stars when only two stars, my
lover's eyes, have utterly confused me?

"To Stargazers" cannot be considered one of Prešeren's best
works. Other than the manipulation of the language—the marvelous
ease with which the poet selected and deployed words, a talent he
must have been born with, for no one in Slovenia could have taught
it to him at that time—little recommends itself to the reader in this
pleasant but shallow verse. We might well wonder why Prešeren
chose to open the section with it.

The answer, if we continue to assume that he arranged the pieces
in his anthology with some purpose in mind, might be found in the
next poem, "V spomin Matija Čopa" [In Memory of Matija Čop,
1846]. Chronology could not have had a bearing on its placement,
nor did genre or subject play a determining role. Prešeren's other
two elegies, to Vodnik and Smolè, were printed side by side in the
lyric section, while the other Slovene tribute to Čop was placed as a
dedication before the epic work "The Baptism on the Savica." And
the German elegy to the poet's friend was not included in *Poems* at
all. Even in purely poetic terms, the convoluted syntax and complex
rhythms of "In Memory of Matija Čop" make an odd contrast with
the simplistic "To Stargazers," to the benefit, it might be added, of
neither poem.

Why does the elegy to Čop follow "To Stargazers"? In this
arrangement Prešeren may have sought to stress the critical role
played by his friend and mentor in helping him to move from the
simple poetry of his early years to the sophisticated verse of the
1830s. Before Čop undertook to guide the "bark of Slovene literature," only hazards and uncertainties awaited the would-be poet.
But with Čop at the helm, the whole civilized world of European
letters was opened to him. Čop was the intermediary of modern
culture; was, as the poem goes on to say, the sower; and the seeds
he planted were now coming to ear in Prešeren's poetry. To stress
Čop's role in his poetic development, then, Prešeren placed "To
Stargazers" first and "In Memory" second in this section.

Like the first poem, however, the elegy cannot be counted among
Prešeren's best poems. He wrote two versions of it, one which is

based on the alternation of long and short syllables, in imitation of Latin and Greek classical verse;[49] and one whose rhythm is based on the alternation of stressed and unstressed syllables. Though he published both, he chose only the latter for inclusion in his anthology. As a very late work the elegy gives testimony to the enduring interest the poet had in metrics, even at the end of his career.[50] The tone of the poem, especially in comparison to the undistilled grief of the German elegy (1835), reveals a more balanced perception of Čop's life and a complete acceptance of the fact of his death. The mature, resigned Prešeren is very much in evidence.

But for all its care, the elegy fails. The syntax is too Latinate. Too many classical references crowd the text. Pomposity replaces the expression of affection. The imagery is unimaginative. Even the phonics of the poem seem "un-Slovene."[51]

If the elegy did not succeed as a poem, at least as a statement of fact it was accurate. For following it are four of Prešeren's master-pieces, written between 1829 and 1832, during the poet's closest friendship with Čop. The first of them is "Nova pisarija" [The New Way to Write, 1831], a long satire on Metelko and his benighted understanding of literature.[52] The poem appeared first in the *Carniolan Bee*, volume 2 (1831) as Prešeren's contribution to the "Ljubljana ABC War." A lengthy dialogue takes place between a "student" who wants to become a Slovene poet, and a "writer" who gives him advice. Among other things the writer tells him to go to the countryside and listen to the peasants speak, for the language of the cities (and the intellectuals) has become too Germanized; to make up words by putting together roots and stems; to purify Slovene of any and all foreign expressions; to sing only what is useful, and to avoid the beautiful; to use only Slovene (i.e., folk) genres, and to avoid romances, ballads, tragedies, sonnets, and the arts; finally to sing only what will benefit the peasant and bourgeois. In ecstasy at this advice, the student exclaims:

> Bog ti zaplati uk, po tvoji volji
> bom pel: gosence kaj na repo varje,
> kak prideluje se krompir narbolji;
> kako odpravljajo se ovcam garje,
> preganjajo ušivim glavam gnide,
> loviti miš' učil bom gospodarje.

God bless you for this lesson, as you wish
I'll sing: how to protect the radishes from bugs,
How one might grow a larger potato,
How to rid sheep of mange
And lousy heads of nits.
I'll teach folks to catch mice.

To this the writer responds: "O, zlati vek zdéj muzam kranjskim
pride!" ("Oh, the golden age will come now to Carniolan muses!").
Despite the light tone, "The New Way to Write" addressed the
most serious literary problem of its day: what course would Slovene
literature take? In the poet's mind the divisions seemed quite clear.
The aspiring poet could follow the Kopitar-Ravnikar-Metelko line,
which promoted a very cautious development of the language and
literature along peasant and didactic lines. Or he could subscribe to
the views of the *Bee* writers and supporters (Prešeren, Kastelic, Čop,
etc.), who felt Slovene could be a vehicle for a sophisticated,
romantic literature, so long as foreign forms and a modicum of
foreign expressions could be used in developing it. In "The New
Way to Write" Prešeren attacks Kopitar's group above all as
"purists" and narrow-minded provincials, who are concerned more
for linguistics than for literature. Only in one area does he agree
with his adversaries: on the necessity of finding a "new Orpheus,"
a national poet who will awaken his people to an awareness of
themselves. He feels, however, that such a person can succeed *only*
if he sings what is beautiful and on par with the rest of European
civilization (for Prešeren this meant what is romantic in form and
content). The audience one must pursue, he implies, is the educated
urban class, who must be won away from German by a Slovene
literature and language that is every bit the equal of German letters
and speech.
     Having provided his view of how Slovene literature should be
nurtured, the poet then gives three examples, three masterpieces
from his canon. The first concerns love, the second life, the third
poetry. They are all three preeminently romantic, yet at the same
time the very personal statement of a poetic genius. They affirm,
more than any mere claim, that Prešeren was in fact the Orpheus of
his people.
     "Prva ljubezen" [First Love, 1832] openly declares its Petrarchan
origin. Written in iambic pentameter with five ottava rima stanzas,
the poem not only mentions the Italian Renaissance poet by name,

but, in a footnote to the first edition of the work in the *Carniolan Bee*, volume 3 (1832), provided the specific reference, as well, to Petrarch's sonnet 3, "It was the day the sun's rays grew dark,"[53] after which "First Love" is clearly modeled. Prešeren opens his statement on first love with the wistful remembrance of the time when he thought he could avoid love's enslavement. He would keep his "heart's freedom" so long as he "stood guard" against love. Then he meets a girl whose attributes outshine all others'. He should have known better—for he has Petrarch's example to fall back on—but he cannot resist looking at her. Without sensing it, he is "wounded," and from then on can find no medicine to heal himself. Unfortunately his obvious lovesickness in no way moves her to pity him, let alone to love him in turn. Do not look at young girls, he concludes: the eyes are thieves of peace, they open the door to love, which conquers then our reason. He who does not pay attention will himself soon be wandering in the same misfortunes as the poet.

"First Love" is perhaps the least tragic of all of Prešeren's serious treatments of love.[54] It predates by at least a year his infatuation for Julija, if we take seriously the poet's account of his meeting her on Holy Saturday 1833. Therefore if its origin is autobiographical, it refers to one of the several flirtations the poet is known to have had up to that time. On the other hand, who the object of Prešeren's affections at the time may have been seems quite irrelevant to us today: the poet sings not of his first beloved, after all, but of first love. Amorousness is his subject, and a stylized, Petrarchan amorousness at that. Such passion is impersonal, hence the less-than-tragic tone of the work.

Varying assessments have been made of the impact of Petrarch on Prešeren's love poetry. Kidrič finds only a superficial Petrarchan imprint, used largely for decorative purposes, in Prešeren's work.[55] Paternu posits a greater role for the Italian poet, both as an intermediary of classical poetry for Prešeren, and as a source which the Slovene exploited flexibly but fully.[56] The early critic Stritar stressed the Petrarchan element in Prešeren's love verse ("Prešeren's love is Petrarch's love, Julija is Laura . . ."),[57] but later critics have backed away from such hard and fixed comparisons.[58]

In "First Love" at least, Petrarch seems to have served Prešeren as a foil for the expression of his own views. Petrarch becomes for him the poet who is consumed by the heat of his ardor for his beloved, the man for whom love constituted the purpose of life.

Such a situation must not be permitted in Prešeren's life, however: reason must not be conquered. But the only way out is to avoid the other sex altogether: do not look, stay chaste. Even in this early poem Prešeren came to the same conclusion he would arrive at after his "Julija period" had passed. The only answer to unrequited love is to live celibately.

In metrical terms "Slovo od mladosti" [Farewell to Youth, 1829], the next poem in the section and by all accounts the greatest single poem in Prešeren's oeuvre, is identical to "First Love," five ottava rima stanzas with hendecasyllabic iambic lines. In terms of its "genre," it is part of the great European romantic tradition of poems on lost youth.[59] The language of this work, which appeared in the first volume of the *Carniolan Bee* (1830) and immediately raised Prešeren in the eyes of the public high above the other poets in the journal, is supple, simple, euphonic, and elegant. Even those who know Slovene cannot now appreciate the revolution Prešeren's language caused in Slovene literature in 1830. But we can note with sympathy Stritar's awe at the poet's ability: after a few attempts of his own, he says, without the support of any native tradition worth speaking of, Prešeren wrote the perfect poem.[60] This perfection lies in the poem's absolutely appropriate and expressive language, which works in perfect harmony with the content.

The poem opens with a reference to the Psalms:[61] "Of my days the better half, / Oh years of my youth, you have quickly, quickly passed." But youth was a troubled time for the poet, sterile and hopeless; nonetheless his heart still sighs for his "dark dawn" (another biblical reference, according to Slodnjak)[62]—may God protect it. Then came awareness, the fruit of experiences of which he partook. Life, he learned, allows for no clear conscience, no good works, no faithful love, no wisdom, justice, or learning. Happiness belongs only to him who can buy it; seemingly worthy things are only lies and deceit.

To apprehend such truths is to wound the heart; but it is youth's happy facility to heal quickly, and still to go on believing in the possibility of earthly happiness. Youth cannot know how easily life dispenses with all hope until it has learned the lesson of age. Therefore the poet's heart will always sigh for his "dark dawn." May God protect it!

The poem explores the contradiction posed in the first stanza. If the poet's youth was indeed so painful, why was it the *better* half of his days and why does he still long for it? The answer given in the next four stanzas is not encouraging: the other half of life contains so many more miseries that youth is better only by comparison. The unrestrained gloom of the poet's mature world view contrasts sharply with the naive utopianism of youth (which "built castles in the clouds" and "laid out green lawns in the deserts"). What makes the poem gloomier, however, is that even this idealistic youth did not belong to the poet. He ate the fruit of awareness early, his childhood was marked not by lawns in the desert but by a few quickly fading flowers. Hence innocence, ignorance, and the capacity for self-delusion were his for only a short time. The poet was deprived of even that minor consolation afforded to others by a normal youth. His tragedy is that he grew up too fast.

We could search Prešeren's biography for evidence of some traumatic childhood experience that might lie at the base of this elegy to a youth cut short. Certainly we should not overlook the mysterious incident at Ribnica, which Prešeren recalled even on his deathbed. We must also be aware that Prešeren wrote "Farewell" precisely at the point where he ended one phase of his life and was entering upon another. He must have been very keenly aware that his own youth had passed. But would we be entitled to believe he foresaw all the misfortunes to come? If we read "Farewell" as a biographical statement, then we must assume an enormous prescience on the poet's part.

Taken as a poetic expression, however, in the European tradition of the poetry of disillusionment with the world,[63] the poem need not be seen as biography in the strict sense. "Farewell to Youth" might be better understood as a pose which, like the Petrarchan pose in the poem before and other poses in other poems, the poet assumed in order to introduce into Slovene literature an important genre of European literature. We are not dealing with a question of sincerity—the poet is not lying to us here anymore than he "lied" to us in "The Unwed Mother" when he spoke as a girl. We do confront in "Farewell to Youth" the first example of the absolute poetic genius of Prešeren, which helped him transcend both the limits of his native tradition *and himself* in order to sing in Slovene what other Europeans were singing. We need not believe literally what the poet tells us about "his" metaphysics in the poem What we must believe and appreciate in the poem is the poet's ability to express those metaphysics in a language which heretofore had been used "to teach folks to catch mice."

The last of these six major poems is entitled "Glosa" [The Glosa,

1832]. The title is a Spanish word for a poetic genre where the lines of one poem are incorporated one by one into another poem, which then explains or elaborates on them.[64] In this case an introductory quatrain—based loosely on Vodnik's poem "My Monument"[65]—provides the last line for each of four ten-line stanzas. The quatrain is a Slovene poet's expression of disgust with the treatment accorded him by his fellow countrymen and by fate. "He lives, he dies without money" sums up the poet's plight.

The first stanza glosses the sentiment that all poets are blind: Homer had to beg in his old age, Ovid lived in exile, Dante, Camões, and Cervantes all suffered to ply their craft. In the second stanza, the average Slovene calls anyone a fool who likes Petrarch, Tasso, the folk poetry of Slovenia, Vodnik, or the *Carniolan Bee*. The third stanza assures us the poet could not find happiness if he went to China, while the fool can stay home and get rich. But the final stanza turns all of this around: the poet cannot stop singing, so let those who must make money go ahead. The poet's castle is the open sky, and no gateman is necessary; the poet's gold is the clear dawn, his silver the dew on the grass. "With this estate, without any difficulty / He lives, he dies without money."

Thus the poet is a free spirit. His commitment to his craft, despite all the shortcomings, sets him apart from the benighted crowds. The reward he receives for fashioning his song is liberation from the tedium which others must face. He can live beyond the walls that encircle others, and perceive what the dazzled (or jaded) eyes of others cannot see. Moreover, as Paternu notes, the poet in "The Glosa" witnesses the "clear dawn," which shines perhaps in answer to the "dark dawn" of youth in the previous poem.[66] Poetry may be the instrument given to the poet (by God or fate or whomever, but still given) with which he can endure the life of poverty, unhappiness, and crushing sensitivity to which he is assigned. Only in singing can he alleviate for a time the pains that wrack him. At the same time, however, "The Glosa" makes clear that, whatever the role of poetry in his life, the poet cannot stop singing even if the personal and social consequences of his song are ruinous.

Up till now in *Poems* Prešeren's verse has displayed very little wittiness. Humor does show through now and then, especially in the early verse (in the later poems the humor turns bitter and sarcastic).[67] But the quick wit, the apt phrase well turned to an opponent's discomfort and the poet's advantage, which contributed to Prešeren's sociability in the taverns of Ljubljana, has not been much in evidence thus far in the anthology. The subsection entitled "Zabavljivi napisi" [Amusing Jottings, 1832-1846] makes up for this lack. It contains the remaining twenty-three items in "Various Poems."

Some of the poems in this section, epigrams all, are obscure to the modern Slovene reader in that they concern specific people and events of Prešeren's time. Unless they are elaborately explained their point is unclear. To the foreigner of course they are even more remote, and, since many of them depend on puns, they are doubly difficult to understand. For the most part they concern the ABC War and the Illyrian Movement. Prešeren's colleagues on the *Carniolan Bee* come in for gentle teasing, the Illyrians on Gaj's *Morning Star* are treated more caustically. And in a singular lapse of taste, Kopitar is castigated viciously in an epigram penned after his death. Paternu maintains that these short works are the beginning of Slovene literary criticism.[68] If so, they are a very modest beginning, which seeks more to entertain than to elucidate. Still, they may have made Slovene literature a topic accessible for discussion by the educated Slovene of the day, and therefore at least in that sense they were successful. Prešeren himself obviously placed relatively little value on them after their usefulness had passed. His final epigram in the section (and one must know that "prešeren" is the Slovene adjective for "proud") says, as if speaking for all its brethren: "Some of us, because we are Prešeren's, dare to be proud ['prešernih'], / [But] these poems show sufficiently how modest our father is."

V *The Ghasels*

One of the principal themes of Prešeren's seven "Gazele" [Ghasels, 1832],[69] the next section of *Poems*, is the immortality afforded to mortals, especially mortal lovers, by poetry.[70] Once a poet has recorded the features of his beloved in his work, she is destined to be remembered for all ages. Even when she dies, her beauty will still be appreciated by men. On the other hand, what drives the poet to compose verse for her is neither his love for her nor her beauty. The other theme of the cycle is that uncertainty forces the poet to sing, perhaps in the hope of clearing up the doubtfulness surrounding his relationship with his beloved, but also unmistakably to record his own doubts and fears about love. The theme of immortality is the explicit motif of this cycle, the theme of uncertainty the implicit one.

Of Prešeren's seven poetic cycles (five in Slovene and two in German), all among the finest poetry he wrote, only this one was not composed in sonnets. Instead the poet chose a genre that had been imported into German literature at the beginning of the nineteenth century and had made its mark there especially in the poetry of Goethe.[71] Originally a genre of classical Arabic and Persian literatures, the ghasel was perfected by the Persian poet Hafiz in the fourteenth century A.D. Ghasels always deal with love, often accompanied by wine drinking. Their structural peculiarity lies in the rhyme scheme: *a a b a c a d a*, etc. While only one word may make the rhyme, often in a ghasel a whole phrase will be repeated along with a rhyming word. Thus the first line and every even-numbered line thereafter can repeat an entire hemistich. No set number of verses is specified for a poem's length.

Many reasons might be adduced why Prešeren felt attracted to this particular form. For one it was popular in Germany, and part of his "program" was to introduce into Slovene the popular forms of other European nations. With its Oriental origin and wine-and-women theme it was quintessentially romantic. Its structure, less rigorous than that of a sonnet, allowed the poet more flexibility in his expression. And yet it had a specific set of structural requirements, the meeting of which would demonstrate once again that the poet and his language were capable of anything other Europeans could do.

The extraordinary intricacy of the poetic and phonic relationships in these poems gives some idea of the care (and talent) with which Prešeren composed his verse. Even more impressive, however, is the great wealth of meanings he managed to weave into his elaborate verbal patterns. Once again in the anthology we encounter what is the most prominent single feature of Prešeren as a poet: his ability to follow complex poetic formulas without sacrificing sense or meaning. Were his language more widely known in the world, Prešeren's rare ability to write thus would long ago have placed him in a class with humanity's great poets.

The cycle opens in ghasel 1 with a metaphor. The poem is a vessel which bears not liquid but sound. The precious sound it contains is his beloved's name. This vessel the poet will take to all Slovenes, and then beyond to all nations. The glow from that cup will continue even after the poet and his mistress are dead. His mistress' name rivals those of all the famous women celebrated in verse, even Laura's.

The vessel reminds us, of course, of a communion chalice, by the preciousness of its contents, its passage among people, its Grail-like glow. Like such a chalice, the poem bearing its unique contents is meant to unite and remind. But to spread his mistress' name, which is the function of the poem just as to distribute the consecrated wine is the function of the chalice, the poet must say that name. And yet, though he names by name other women, his own beloved's name he leaves unsaid. Just why her name is ineffable he does not reveal, although such a quality belongs to divinity, and in that regard the metaphor of the poem as a holy chalice is maintained. Failure to mention her name, however, charges the first ghasel with much emotional tension.

Ghasel 2 is metrically distinct from the rest of the cycle, in that it is made up of iambs instead of the trochees of the other ghasels. The poet's pose is different here as well: he is not worshipful, as in ghasel 1, nor despairing nor imploring nor self-vindicating as in the others. He is simply confused. First his mistress is warm, then she is cold; now indifferent, now jealous. Does she love him or dislike him? The last line, though syntactically joined to the next-to-the-last line, is metrically apart—it is trochaic, like all the other poems. It asks: "How I can please you, I, a wretch, do not know" ("ne vem"), and then the word "know" ("ve") is repeated in the third ghasel ten times.

What is known in ghasel 3 is, however, that the poet loves his mistress, *not* how he might please her. He catalogs all of creation: night and dawn, morning, noon, and evening, the walls of his room, the noise of the city, a rose, a bird, the sill of her door, a stone, the path to her. "All created matter knows what my beloved girl will neither know nor hear from me / Nor believe, that I love her." Once again Prešeren has used a religious setting—the poem reads like a canticle—to deliver a plea that his beloved acknowledge and accept his love. The exaltation created by the lengthy parallelism of the poem's structure leads not to fulfillment but to disappointment. The inference we draw is that the poet is even more unsure of his mistress' love now than in ghasel 2.

Ghasel 4, the central poem, contains his confession. He ascribes the coldness of his beloved to the scandalous rumors which other women have circulated about him. Again his mistress appears, as in 2, to be jealous—at least a more hopeful reaction to him than indifference. And he elaborately explains that until one has seen a rose, violets seem pretty enough; until one has heard a nightingale,

the song of lesser birds suffices. He admits to having looked at other
girls, but now that he has seen the sun, all such shadows have been
driven from his eyes.

Sight and sound play a contrasting duet in these first four poems.
In ghasel 1, the precious item the poems offer is the sound of his
mistress' name. In 2, her glances confuse the poet; his looking at
other girls angers her. In 3 he writes: "In my poems there is the
continual, selfsame statement, that I love her." And in 4, the chatter
of other women has turned his mistress against him; he asks her to
listen to him. By the same token, she has blinded him, like the sun,
to other girls. Thus visual communication between poet and loved
one is unreliable, even harmful. Only his poetry conveys the truth.
But if he can speak to her in that fashion, how is she to respond to
him? The answer is, by reading his poetry, thereby allowing him to
please her (the answer to the question posed in 2), and assuring him
of her affection for him (the question implicitly posed in 3). These
answers are elaborated in the remaining ghasels.

Ghasel 5 reminds the girl of the classical notion that "life is short,
art long." Reiterating the imagery of the earlier poems, he writes:
"Hear this poor poet whom your glance has wounded." Then he
goes on to say that Helen's beauty and the Trojans' sacrifice are
remembered thanks only to poetry. The time of life is short, so he
counsels haste. It is as if the poet were Homer, blinded by his lover's
beauty. She should hurry so that he can immortalize her the way
Homer did Helen. What should she do? Read his poetry.

Ghasel 6 makes this response quite clear. Like the seedling, the
farmer, the nomad, the merchant, or the soldier, no one knows if
what he does today will bring a suitable reward tomorrow. Neither
does the "poet of these little ghasels" know whether his mistress
will read them, or, if she does, whether she will understand that she
was their cause. Her acceptance of his work becomes paramount for
him. He composes for her on faith, as others plant trees; his poetry
will not be complete unless (or until) she reads it. With little
difficulty one can extend the poet's meaning here beyond the
merely amatory. Prešeren's chief concern, it would seem from these
poems, was to reach as many Slovenes as possible, to gather them
all together in the "communion" of his poetry so that a nation
might emerge from scattered tribes. Therefore his plea to his
mistress should be seen as a plea to the nation to appreciate the
fruits of his labor by reading them. The odds against Prešeren (and

any other poet at the time for that matter) were enormous: dialectal distinctions, censorship, the educated public's disdain of Slovene and preference for foreign things, the poverty of the native tradition, the limited resources for disseminating Slovene books, the small audience. Ghasel 6 is the poet's credo that, despite all, he will be appreciated. It is also a challenge, that he has done all he can and that now others must act in response.

Ghasel 7, the last, is a statement of principle, first about these several poems, and second about the poet's art in general. In it he mentions the reactions to his verse. Some like it, but more criticize it for not being folklike or classical, still others for its excessive innocence or disquieting eroticism. Even those whom the sound of the ghasels might have pleased are dissatisfied. But the poet has one goal only: to please his beloved. He has not consulted with any others.

It is fairly obvious that this last ghasel is not what it appears to be at first sight. It is not a survey of reactions to his poems; Prešeren's point is not to defend the ghasels. Rather he is seeking the freedom he needs to employ whatever means necessary to achieve his poetic goal. Here that goal is giving pleasure to his beloved. But whatever it might be, he pleads for the right to pursue it. The poet alone must be responsible for what he writes—even when, as he implies, the criticism comes from friendly sources.[72] His sensibility alone must make the poetic judgments, and only the sensibility of his "beloved"—the Slovene reading public as much as his mistress—can assert whether "she" is pleased or not.

Placed where they are in his anthology Prešeren's seven ghasels form ultimately a request to the reader: read on, with an open mind. The explicit and implicit themes of the cycle—poetry as a means to immortality for his beloved, uncertainty as the prod for the poet to write—are subsumed under the general theses that poetry crystallizes the nation and that the poet, working freely, is the only one capable of judging his own product. This elevation of the ghasel cycle above the personal and onto the level of the national is clear by the final poem, where only once does the poet refer to his beloved. Perhaps the post's mistress had in real life good reason to be jealous of him. For from these poems it is evident she had to share his affections not with other women, but with poetry itself and with his growing awareness of himself as the national poet of the Slovenes.

VI *Sonnets*

In all Prešeren composed forty-six Slovene sonnets that have come down to us. By omitting only four of them from the anthology he gave ample proof of the high regard with which he held his work in this genre. The sonnet, in fact, was Prešeren's preferred form. In it he wrote his best poetry. His reputation is based largely on the sonnet cycles that crown the last part of the anthology.

In his notes to F. L. Čelakovský's laudatory review of the *Carniolan Bee*'s first three volumes, Matija Čop defends Prešeren's use of the sonnet against the traditionalists who favored the verse forms used by Valentin Vodnik.[73] Why not use the best verse forms Europe has to offer? If other nations can borrow, why not the Slovenes too? Why not select the most beautiful of all poetic forms, the sonnet, which has been in use in European literatures since the thirteenth century? Čop then gives a brief and selective history of sonnet use in Europe, beginning with the Italian masters (Dante, Petrarch, later Tasso), continuing with Lope de Vega, Camões, Shakespeare, Milton, Opitz, Fleming, Bürger, A. W. von Schlegel, the Dalmatian Dinko Ranjina, the Poles Jan Kochanowski, Mikołaj Sęp-Szarzyński, and Adam Mickiewicz, and finishing with "the greatest living Czech poet, Jan Kollár." As Prešeren's contribution to the genre, Čop mentions the "Love Sonnets" of volumes 2 and 3 of the *Bee*.

Of all these potential sources for Prešeren's sonnetry, only three played a truly important role. Prešeren could read Italian, and knew well especially the sonnets of Petrarch. The poet not only used Petrarch as a model in both form and theme, but on occasion used the Italian poet as a subject himself, sometimes in direct references. Prešeren was also well acquainted with German literature in the original. Particularly the poets and writers of the Silesian and Jena "Schools"—the brothers Schlegel, who prescribed "proper" sonnet form, Novalis, Opitz, Fleming—informed his views of German sonnetry. Last but perhaps most important for subject matter were the sonnets of Jan Kollár. Prešeren knew no Czech, so that he had to rely on others for information about Kollár's most famous sonnet cycle, *The Daughter of Sláva*. But by 1832, Sir John Bowring had published his English translations of many sonnets from the cycle,[74] giving Prešeren an almost firsthand look at Kollár's work and profoundly influencing him in the process.[75]

Perhaps even more influential than the literary sources which

Prešeren could and did consult directly were those critical sources to which he turned for technical information on sonnets. The first of these was the book *Introduction to Popular Poetry* (1794) by Giambattista Bisso,[76] the second were the treatises of A. W. von Schlegel entitled *Lectures on Literature and Art* (1802 and 1803),[77] and the third was the "giant of learning," Čop himself, who wrote nothing about his understanding of the sonnet other than what was cited above, but who undoubtedly was Prešeren's chief intermediary in explicating the genre. From these sources, especially Schlegel and Čop, Prešeren acquired an understanding of the potential of the sonnet form which, beginning in 1830, he translated into the first great sonnets ever written in Slovene.[78]

For compactness and effectiveness, the fourteen lines of iambic pentameter known as a sonnet have few rivals.[79] The Petrarchan sonnet especially, with its intertwining rhymes, has become so popular that it has spread throughout the world, and remained lively for more than six centuries. The effectiveness of the sonnet can in part be attributed to its division into two parts, a section consisting usually of the first eight lines unified by only two rhymes (*a b b a   a b b a*   or   *a b a b   a b a b*) and a section composed of the last six lines, rhymed in terza rima fashion (*c d c   d c d*) or with three rhymes (*c d e   c d e*) (other rhyme schemes are also possible). As a result of the structure a progression of thought is inherent in every well-written sonnet. That is, a problem or situation is proposed in the octain and resolved or explained in the sextain. The rhyme scheme unifies the expression in each part on the one hand, and separates the two parts on the other hand, giving a clear sense of movement from one integral unit to another. The limited number of syllables available to the poet—from 140 to 154, depending on whether he uses decasyllabic or hendecasyllabic lines, or a combination of the two—forces upon him the greatest spareness of expression. One consequence of this constraint is that some languages, especially those with shorter words, like Slovene, Italian, and English, are more innately suited to the rigors of the sonnet form than other languages with longer words, like German and Russian, because they can accommodate more cognitively functional units—words—within the sonnet's prescribed limits.

In the sonnet, then, Prešeren and Čop found a form in many ways ideal for their purposes. Successful sonnetry in Slovene would raise that language to the level of the other European languages successfully using the form. Slovene seemed, for its lexical and phonetic

qualities, capable of use in the sonnet form, and just as critical, the
demands of this form were ideally suited to the controlled genius of
Prešeren, which excelled when placed in the narrowest of confines.

A *"Love Sonnets"*

As far as we know, Prešeren's first sonnets were written in 1830
and published in 1831 and 1832. Originally they were to bear a
collective title of "Ljubeznjeni sonetje" [Love Sonnets] but this the
poet later deleted. They were, however, placed together by the poet
as the first five pieces of the sonnet section of his *Poems*, and can
thus still be considered as a group.

The first one, "Očetov naših imenitne dela" [The famous deeds
of our fathers], is divided, like all the remainder in this section, into
two quatrains and two tercets. As in all the other quatrains, the
rhyme scheme is the conventional *a b b a   a b b a*. Only the tercets'
rhymes differ from sonnet to sonnet. In the first it is *c d e   c d e*.
The point of the quatrains is that the poetry of "our [i.e., Slovene]
Homers" should tell about the famous events in our national history.
This poet's strings are too weak, however (he goes on to say in the
tercets) to sing of battles. He sings instead of the beauties of Slovene
women and his pitiless mistress. He sings for everyone the misfortunes of his love and "What a wretch he is, whom the arrow / Shot
from those heavenly eyes has pierced."

Having refrained from titling them thus, the poet nonetheless
makes clear from the outset that these are indeed sonnets of love.
Cupid's arrow has transfixed him, so he must tell everyone why he
is miserable: his beloved does not return his love. Yet the poet is
hardly docile, in fact, he is somewhat sarcastic. He will leave it to
the "Homers"—the plural is meant to be demeaning—to sing
things his strings are "too weak" to sing, yet he sings exactly martial
things for fully half of the sonnet (lines 1-7). Thus by "too weak" he
does not mean "incapable" but presumably "too delicate." Having
excluded himself from the circle of poor Slovene poets, he goes on
to establish who he is: the heartsick lover stroking his lyre in honor
of his hardhearted "girl" and all beautiful women. These details are
intended to produce a Renaissance aura around the poet, to identify
him with Beatrice's or Laura's admirers. From the outset the poet's
position is clear.

The second sonnet, "Vrh sonca sije soncov cela čeda" [A flock of
suns above the sun does shine], displays clearly Petrarchan imagery
and diction.[80] The poet says the earth, though in love with the sun,

still looks at the stars (the flock of suns) at night. But when day breaks, the earth returns to the fixed contemplation of its sun. So too the poet, who looks at the girls of Ljubljana, that are as numerous as stars, until his "sun," the beloved, appears and makes him blind to all the others.

Once again the poet's tone is less than submissive. This sonnet is addressed to the "blooming-cheeked" girls of Ljubljana, not to the beloved, who is referred to only in the third person. The poet is, as it were, apologizing to them for his neglect of their stellar beauty. He explains that he is blinded by the radiance of another, and infatuated. Rather diplomatically he avoids responsibility for his neglect of the Ljubljana ladies by making himself the passive victim of his beloved's overpowering attributes (note even the passive voice in lines 12 and 14). But the point is still valid: he "looks happily" (present tense) at the girls whenever he has a chance. In love he may be, but he is not yet completely under the thumb of his "girl."

In the third sonnet in this cycle, "Tak kakor hrepeni oko čolnarja" [As the eye of the sailor longs to see], a sailor longs to catch sight of Castor and Pollux rising, for he knows then that the end of bad weather is at hand and peace will soon again reign on the sea. So, too, the poet awaits the rays from his beloved's eyes, for even if she will not still his storm for him, nonetheless "the sky around my boat will straightaway grow clear."

As in the first sonnet, in the third sonnet too the poet addresses his mistress directly. But this time he addresses no one else (unlike the first, where he also spoke to "everyone"). Thus sonnet 3 is more intimate, and bears no trace either of the poet's sarcasm or his boldness. The sailor motif, as we have seen in the anthology thus far ("The Sailor" and "The Fisherman"), Prešeren did not use lightly: the sea is a place where questions of life and death are decided. On the sea man has the least control over the forces of nature, he is most dependent upon fate to bring him to safety again. Sonnet 3 records the poet's realization of his peril. His "bark" is in a most precarious position. And he has been reduced to begging for a mere glance from his beloved to save his soul. Hopes that she might deign to love him have been, it seems, completely dismissed. The poet can expect no peace or happiness from his love for his girl.

The fourth sonnet, "Dve sestri videle so zmoti vdane" [My eyes, given over to error, have seen two sisters] was not originally published with sonnets 1-3 and 5, but a year later, in the third volume of the *Bee*. Yet for his anthology of 1846 Prešeren placed it

fourth of the five "Love Sonnets." Its positioning seems in part due
to its subject matter.

The "two sisters" of the first line, one tall, the other short, are the
"flower of beauty" and "the pride of Ljubljana." But the poet runs
from them as the deer who was once wounded by hunters runs from
them again, mindful of her former pain. The poet runs because once
he was wounded by Cupid's arrow and by Cupid's mother; and
these two sisters remind him of two gods, the shorter of Amor
(Cupid), and the taller of Venus (his mother).

Once again the poet returns to addressing "everyone" ("If you all
ask me . . ."). Once again the tone of the poem is lighter, with the
poet's bad eyesight, the short and the tall sisters (the contrast is
humorous), the resemblance of one of them to cherubic Cupid, even
the poet's running away. The peril of sonnet 3 seems to have
disappeared now. The poet is away from the sea and back in
Ljubljana. Perhaps he is even back to looking at other girls again.
His former passion has become merely "an old wound"; he seems
quite determined to avoid inflicting on himself any new ones.

The lightening of the tone is taken to the point of open humor in
the last of the "Love Sonnets," "Kupido! ti in tvoja lepa starka"
[Cupid, you and your pretty parent]. Obviously the poet has decided
to confront the pair face-to-face rather than run like a deer.
The rhyme scheme of the tercets here is pure Italian terza rima,
c d c d c d, but the point and form are anti-Petrarchan.

Unlike all the other sonnets the fifth offers no contrast between
the quatrains and the tercets. Rather there is the continuous
development of one thought: the poet refuses to be used, as "poor
Petrarch" was, by Cupid and his mother. He wants compensation if
he sings their praises. But if they do not "pay off" by giving him the
girl he seeks, then for the rest of his life he will busy himself with
his legal practice, spend time with his friends, and use wine to drive
off the "clouds of care." What, he asks, did his "poetic vein" ever
net him anyway? By the fifth sonnet then the poet has recovered
from the "arrow loosed from the eyes of his beloved" in the first
sonnet. He has regained the presence of mind and wit lost in the
second sonnet. He no longer worries about imminent death and
peril, as in the third sonnet. And he even finds courage to face up to
love and renounce it, unlike the fourth sonnet. "Love," he writes,
"will no longer lead me by the nose."

Unfortunately for Prešeren, he underestimated the power of love.
Very soon after writing the "Love Sonnets" he composed "First

·Love," that tribute to love's omnipotence. In the first printed version of 1832, he prefaced it with a doublet from the Latin poet Propertius, which in effect signaled that the happy resignation of the "Love Sonnets" was but a passing phase in his desperate quest for true love: "You who used to say no woman could harm you any more / Have spoken too soon: that wit of yours has failed you."[81]

As if to make the same point in the anthology, Prešeren followed his "Love Sonnets" with a much later, explicitly Petrarchan, and very pessimistic sonnet, "Je od vesel'ga časa teklo leto" [The twice nine hundred and thirty-third year has passed since that happy time]. The date of composition of this piece is uncertain. The text seems to imply 1833, but critics argue with some merit for a much later date, perhaps 1838-1839.[82] In any event the poet's attitude has changed completely. The humor and resignation have disappeared. Once again the poet is cast as "poor Petrarch," on whose works moreover he models this sonnet quite openly.[83] The fateful moment of his falling in love has undone him completely. At about ten o'clock, on Saturday in Holy Week 1833, he saw two eyes of pure flame. A spark fell on his heart from them, and no power can ever put it out.

> Je od vesel'ga časa teklo leto,
> kar v Bétlehemu angelcov hozana
> je oznanila, de je noč končana,
> dvakrat devetsto triintrideseto.
>
> Bil vel'ki teden je; v saboto sveto,
> ko vabi molit božji grob kristjana,
> po cerkvah tvojih hodil sem, Ljubljana!
> v Trnovo, tje sem uro šel deseto.
>
> Trnovo! kraj nesrečnega imena;
> tam meni je gorje bilo rojeno
> od dveh očesov čistega plamena.
>
> Ko je stopila v cerkev razsvetljeno,
> v srcé mi padla iskra je ognjena,
> ki ugásnit' se ne da z močjo nobeno.
>
> From that happy time have flowed
> As in Bethlehem the angels' cry
> Announced the night was o'er,
> Twice nine hundred and thirty-three years.

It was Holy Week; on Holy Saturday
As God's grave summons the Christian to prayer,
I wandered through your churches, Ljubljana!
To Trnovo I went at about ten o'clock.

Trnovo! Sad-named place;
There grief was born for me
From two eyes of pure flame.

When she entered the bright church,
A fiery spark fell upon my soul,
Which no power at all can put out.

In the anthology this sonnet also acts as a transition between the joy of the "Love Sonnets" and the lovesickness of Prešeren's greatest achievement, "A Wreath of Sonnets," which follows. It is both the epilogue of the five love sonnets and the prologue of the fifteen wreath sonnets. Moreover, it might be the epilogue of all of Prešeren's Slovene sonnets, for after 1837 Prešeren returned only twice—both times in German—to the sonnet form. If in fact "Twice nine hundred . . ." is the poet's last Slovene sonnet, then we might understand it as a turning point in the poet's life, too. For the "fiery spark . . . which no power at all can put out," as he described his love for Julija, was indeed extinguished by 1838-1839. The poet abandoned his last hope of winning Julija's affections, and perhaps of winning a completely satisfying love in general. And, whether as the result of a conscious decision to stop, or simply because he had lost the inspiration, he ceased writing in the genre in which he had created the still unrivaled master poems of Slovene literature.

B   "A Wreath of Sonnets"

The version of "Sonetni venec" [A Wreath of Sonnets, 1833] which appeared in the anthology of 1846 differs linguistically and stylistically from the original version, which was published as a special supplement to the *Illyrian List* on 22 February 1834.[84] The sense of both versions is by and large the same, however. Since the later text not only represents the poet's final word on his poem, but also appears to be more successful artistically, we will consider only that version here. But it should be kept in mind that the "Wreath" is a product of both the poet's youthful period and his most mature writing. It is in fact a synthesis of his entire creative life.

One of the virtues of the sonnet form can also be construed as a shortcoming. Often the extreme economy of expression required by the form necessitates an abbreviated thought. For the poet who wishes to say more and yet still retain the sonnet form for its other virtues, the answer to the problem of brevity has been the sonnet cycle, a grouping of several sonnets much like the stanzas of an ordinary poem, with the difference that in the sonnet cycle, each sonnet maintains its own integrity of expression as well.[85]

A tension necessarily exists in such a cycle between the individual parts and the whole they comprise. If each sonnet is too individualized, then the whole lacks coherence. If the sonnets lack individuality for the sake of the larger point, however, then the purpose of using sonnets is lost. They become fourteen-line stanzas in a large poem. One way to resolve this tension to the benefit of both the whole and the parts has been to introduce some specific structural requirements into the arrangement of the individual sonnets, so that their individuality becomes a function of structure as well as sense, giving the poet thereby more latitude in working the sense of each sonnet into the broader meaning of the poem. One type of arrangement is the "crown of sonnets," whose exemplar in English are the "Holy Sonnets" of John Donne.

Another such arrangement is the "Wreath of Sonnets," an invention of the literary academy of Siena (Accademia degl'Intronati), a Renaissance institution which legislated matters of form and usage in Italian. Prešeren probably learned of their sonnet cycle through a German-language text on Italian grammar (Karl Ludwig Fernow's *Italian Grammar*, editions of 1804 and 1811),[86] which describes the "wreath" as a cycle of fourteen sonnets, the last line of each furnishing the first line of the following sonnet (the fourteenth gives the first line of the first, hence closing the "wreath"). Moreover, the first line of each sonnet, when read together, forms a fifteenth, or "master sonnet." To these very demanding requirements Prešeren added a further refinement: an acrostic. That is, in his wreath the first letter of each line in the master sonnet spells out the name of his beloved ("Primicovi Julji," "To Julija Primic").[87]

The difficulty of constructing a wreath of sonnets is such that no poet before or after Prešeren has ever done one with the success even approximating the Slovene poet's.[88] In "A Wreath of Sonnets" Prešeren managed to harmonize his form with an extraordinarily sophisticated content, so that the thought progresses throughout the work and is summarized without distortions in syntax or logic in the master sonnet. We may attribute his success here to his facility with rhyme and meter, his superb command of the resources of his native language, and, as we have noted above, his delight in the rigors of form. By composing a wreath, moreover, a feat rarely accomplished in even the most developed literatures of Europe, Prešeren secured the formal triumph of Slovene as a literary vehicle. And he delivered the final blow to Kopitar's and others' arguments about the need to nurture Slovene on peasant forms.

The first sonnet of the cycle, "Your poet is weaving the Slovenes a new wreath,"[89] is, like all the rest, in pure Petrarchan form: iambic pentameter, feminine rhyme, *a b b a   a b b a* in the quatrains and terza rima *c d c   d c d* in the tercets. It serves as an introduction to the cycle, explaining both the structure and the poet's reason for writing. For the poet the most important feature of the wreath is its intertwining. All the harmonies arise from and return to the same source, the master sonnet. Analogously his beloved is, he says, the master sonnet of his life: "All thoughts arise from this one love."

Yet from the very beginning the poet speaks of his love as unhappy and unrequited. The poem is a monument not only to his beloved, but also to his wounds. All his waking hours are obsessed by thoughts of love. As in so many of the poems preceding the "Wreath," death makes its appearance early on and in close association with the poet's love. But poetry triumphs over it, because not even death can still the poet's voice.

Two other points are also made in this first sonnet. The poet says he is weaving a "new wreath." Slodnjak argues convincingly that the implied other "wreath" is the "Ghasels," the poet's earlier cycle.[90] There the poet in the first ghasel stressed that "his song was the vessel of his beloved's name." In the "Wreath" the acrostic containing Julija's name makes this literally so. Moreover, the very elements that comprise the "Ghasels," erotic and poetic, are going to be reconsidered here, and intertwined in a new way. The other point of sonnet 1 has to do with weaving the wreath "for Slovenes." Paternu views the "Wreath" as a balm which Prešeren prepared to heal the wounds inflicted by the Ljubljana ABC War.[91] Instead of fighting jejune battles over orthography, poets were again composing poetry. Therefore the "Wreath" has a national pupose as well as a personal one: to create for Slovenes something unique and to overcome the hostilities of the preceding years. Sonnet 1 proffers the poetic, erotic, and patriotic strands Prešeren is going to weave into a new wreath.[92]

The second sonnet, "A monument to my wounds and to your praise," continues to develop the themes of the "Wreath." Death and sleep alone allay the poet's erotic yearnings. But if these poems become a monument to remind Slovene girls to love faithfully and less proudly, then the pain that causes them to be written will have been somewhat justified. And if better times and better poets should someday appear in Slovenia, still the poet hopes these poems will remain alive, for they are the original flowerings of his own heart.

The note of resignation struck here—it is hopeless to think his mistress might be softened by these poems—is balanced by the hope of a kind of immortality. In essence the poet says that if he cannot get justice here and now, then at least ultimately he might receive just reward for his love and for his poetry. The image of the seed blossoming forth into the bud, used before in Ghasel 6, reappears here, for the first but not the last time in the "Wreath." Its meaning is clear. If the poet's relationship with his mistress is to remain sterile, then his urge to create will have to burst forth elsewhere, for example, in his poetry. The resignation of the poet to lovelessness loses some of its bitterness thanks to his conviction that poetry is another, equally if not even more valid, way to gain immortality than through children.

Due to the structure of repeating lines, the bud image recurs in the third sonnet, "Forth from my heart [the roses] have come to bud." Silence is impossible for the poet to maintain, yet the poet, like Tasso, fears to upset his beloved by singing his misery out loud. So his poems "reveal love secretly." Silence would equal sterility, which the poet cannot endure; outright revelation would offend his mistress. The only recourse is to declare his feelings in verse, thus allaying them by speaking them out, yet hiding them by poeticizing them.

Sonnet 4, perhaps the loveliest in the cycle, "My poems' moist-flowering little roses," likens the poet to a garden, "where love now sows elegies," and his mistress to the sun, who should but will not shine on him. Therefore, he concludes, the songs he has composed in her honor are from a sunless place, and pale.

The peculiar beauty of his sonnet—and this is true to some extent of all of Prešeren's major poems—defies translation. For its aesthetic effect the poem relies on the pithiness and terseness of Prešeren's phrases, which always seem to find the right word or create one where necessary (like "mokrócvetéče," "moist-flowering," in the first line). Assonance and alliteration play a definitive role everywhere: they imbue each verse with an irresistible flow. For example,

"kjer seje zdéj ljubezen elegije" ("where love now sows elegies")
moves from "je" to "eje" to "éj" to "é" and finally to "í," with
increasingly tighter articulation of the stressed vowel; or "ne v
krajih, kjer plesavk vrstà se vije" ("not in lands where the women's
dance line twists") repeats the *v* (but only visually, for it is pro-
nounced three different ways, as *w*, *u*, and only finally as *v*), and alli-
terates the *r* (as consonant and vowel), *k*, *j*, and *s*, thus intertwining
the entire verse in repeating sounds (*v-k-r-j k-j-r s-v-k v-r-s s-v-j*).
The rhymes are rich and varied, the vocabulary elegantly simple.
Perhaps only the imagery of this sonnet (and of the entire
"Wreath") is "pale," to use the poet's word, because by and large it
is conventional. But in a literature like Slovene, which until Prešeren
lacked even the most hackneyed topoi of world literature, conven-
tionality itself may have been a virtue. In any event the pale
metaphors do not stand in the way of the continued enjoyment of
the verse to the present day, an enjoyment based solidly on
Prešeren's acoustical, linguistic, and structural genius as a poet.

Sonnet 5, "They are not from places where the sun shines,"
makes extensive use of anaphora to depict the poet's fantasies. His
poems are not from places where good things happen: where the
beloved looks at him, his care dies, his pains are forgotten, where
there is joy, no internal dissension, where poetry comes from an
overflowing heart and arouses sweet harmonies, where buds are
nurtured by love and nobility. His poems are rather from places
where soft winds do not blow.

In this sonnet the poet revels in a vision of what might have been,
had he found a mutual love. The progression in his involvement
with that fantasy from line to line is breathtaking. First, he is merely
in the same place as his beloved, then she looks at him, then smiles
at him, then satisfies his "internal dissension" (yields to him?), then
bears with him their offspring ("beautiful buds"). The concluding
image, that his songs lack soft winds, indeed confirms a kind of
breathlessness induced no doubt by his ardor. For the moment his
erotic impulse is exhausted, however, by these fantasies. The
following sonnet therefore takes up a different strand of the
"Wreath."[93]

Since "They have always lacked the soft winds," the poet's songs
could not do proper homage to the Slovene muses, for fear that the
poet's beloved and other young Slovene women, who could speak
German, would disdain this product of the local Parnassus. The
masses of Slovenes, says sonnet 6, prefer foreign muses to Slovene

ones. The efforts of Slovene poets, then, are like small roses blooming on the top of huge glaciers.

Clearly the poet is not excusing his use of the native tongue here. He is bemoaning the icy indifference of his countrymen to Slovene and the consequent underdeveloped state of Slovene letters. The national-cultural issue—the patriotic theme—has now been broached. Its internal antagonism arises from the clash between language and literature (Slovene) and custom and fashion (Austro-German). The former lack respectability. It is the poet's hope to give them some.

But to move the hearts of an entire nation, the poet must become an Orpheus, the mythical poet who with his singing pacified the barbarians of Thrace. Sonnet 7, "Around them have arisen rugged peaks," makes a fervent supplication for just such an event, the appearance of a Slovene Orpheus whose song would "melt the hearts of Carniola's sons and all the Slovene tribes roundabout." It would cause Slovenes to honor their land, it would heal their divisions and reunite all those who speak the language into one nation.

Here the poet is being disingenuous. He gives no hint that he considers himself to be this Orpheus. And yet of course he is acting in an Orpheic way. He wants his poetry to unite the country and calm its conflicts. He is seeking to give dignity to a language which, until his time, was relegated to catechisms and agricultural tracts. Why he hesitates to assume the Orpheic mantle is revealed in the last tercet: Orpheus's songs were sweet and made the people happy. They calmed the dissension—"prepir" in Slovene, the very same word used in sonnet 5 to describe Prešeren's turbulent internal state. The Slovene poet cannot do the same, much as he would like to, for his lack of internal calm prevents his singing to achieve national tranquility.

Furthermore, as sonnet 8, "The chill homes of angry storms," makes clear, Slovenia is hardly Thrace. The history of the country is one of long subjugation and unsuccessful revolts against foreign rulers. The people have forgotten what honor, glory, happiness mean. Whatever few roses still grow on the slopes of the Slovene Parnassus have not been nurtured, says the poet, by joy or pride: "Sighs and tears have nourished them."

The poet cannot be an Orpheus for two reasons. He himself is incapable of happy poems, and the people would not know how to receive the efforts in any event. Only one avenue seems open to

him: to sing in the elegiac tones that most closely reproduce the
mournful history of his people. For this he is especially suited, for
he himself is miserable, too.

Sonnet 9, "Sighs and tears have nourished them," confirms this
point. The "little roses of Parnassus" that belong to the poet have
been nurtured by his love for his mistress and his country. But the
thoughts that Slovenes do not love their motherland and that his
mistress will never love him afflict him with renewed vigor:

> Željé rodile so prehrepeneče,
> de s tvojim moje bi ime slovelo
> domače pesmi milo se glaseče,
>
> željé, de zbudil bi Slovenš'no célo,
> de bi vrnili k nam se časi sreče,
> jim moč so dale rasti nevesélo.
>
> All the reward I wished for was that you
> With me a poet's timeless fame might share,
> That native songs our poignant tale might bear;
>
> That all Slovenes should waken and that true
> Content and joy might come. Despite my care,
> Frail growth these blossoms had, so sad and few.

The union of his erotic longings with his patriotic feeling is made
explicit in this sonnet. It provides the stimulus, lacking in love alone
or patriotism alone, for him to continue to write.

Vital forces thus restored, the poet in sonnet 10, "[They] gave
them unhappy power to grow," turns to the poetic theme for the
rest of the "Wreath." Having reported in sonnet 8 some national
history, he now gives some of the personal history of his love for his
mistress. He compares it to a rose "seduced" by the sun of a warm
February. The flower grows happily for a while until the "poisoned
hail" and snow come again to cover the fields. So too had the sparks
from his beloved's eyes brought his love to bud. But those buds
were premature, and darkness has settled on them again.

Seduced, deluded, benighted, even poisoned, the poet responds
bitterly as he recalls the course of his unhappy love. Perhaps with
such a bleak picture of his condition he hoped to stir some pity in
his mistress' heart. More probably, however—in that he has given

up on her earlier in the poem—he is here simply surrendering to the despair that lovelessness brings. For him this sonnet is the darkest spot in the "Wreath." It is almost existentialist in the hopelessness of his situation, its lack of exits. Nor is relief in sight.

From the historical perspective of sonnet 10 the poet moves to the present "reality" (of course, poetic) of sonnet 11, "The forces of dark hours have obliterated them." Pursued by the furies of his despair, he would flee like Orestes to some sanctuary for relief from the disgust he feels with life. His mistress' love would have been the restorative for him. But that dream flees as quickly as a flash of lightning, leaving the night darker yet. How can his poetry be anything but pale?

Sonnets 10 and 11 present the poet at his very nadir. He is driven by an obsessive love and cannot find anyone to relieve him of it. Then in the moment of his deepest despair, at the very darkest hour of the night, the poet gives birth to his poems. They are conceived in agony and born in darkness; wretchedness is their birthmark. The sonnet not only records this moment, but also defends the "child." For the poet answers the implied questions: "Why are these songs so dreary?" and "How can you present such pale flowers to your mistress?"

In his last ghasel, Prešeren also had undertaken to defend his poems—recognizing their pallid quality—for their novelty and ingenuity. He had concluded there that he wrote what he wrote with only one goal in mind: to please his mistress. In the "Wreath," however, pleasing his mistress no longer represents his aim. The purpose of his poetry is: to record his misery; by speaking it out perhaps to exorcise it; and to create in the process something new for his nation. If the result of his creation does not happen to conform to his mistress' taste—or perhaps by implication to anyone's taste—then the poet assumes no responsibility for that. At the very least, sonnet 11 represents the liberation of the poet, in so many other ways enslaved by love, from the artistic oppression of his unappreciative readers. For the as yet quite young Slovene literature, sonnet 11 was a veritable declaration of independence.

The tone of sonnet 12, "Look, that is why their flowers are so pale!" brightens considerably as the poet considers again the possibility that his mistress might take pity on him. Comparing his poetry to a rose that has grown up in a ruin among thorns, he says it will blossom bountifully if only someone will transplant it to a proper flower bed. If she wants prettier flowers than these pale ones he gives her here, then the poet's mistress must bestow the rays of her eyes on them again.

This sonnet continues the poetic manifesto of the last one. The poet, having established his right to independence for his poetry, nonetheless admits his need for recognition and support. He claims that his poetry will be more beautiful if he can compose it within the framework of an accepting society.

The mark of the thirteenth sonnet, "Send them the dear rays from your eyes," is the future tense. If his mistress cooperates, the poet says, then the chains of care will fall away, the irons will drop off, the wounds will heal, his face will brighten, hope will grow green again in his heart, sweet words will come to his lips, his heart will revive, and a more joyful flower will blossom in his verse. In a word, everything the poet wants will be his. He will achieve a personal utopia.

This imagery continues into the fourteenth sonnet of the cycle, "And they will bloom anew more joyously." But here the vision is extended to the nation. In the conventional terms of the idyll he describes the paradise that awaits the land thus renewed by his mistress' smile and his happy poetry: spring, a warm sun, bees, shepherds, nightingales in oak groves. "Joy pervades all of nature." The two quatrains conclude the poet's fantasies as he and all mankind are restored to a garden of delight.

But just as these gardens and their euphoric inhabitants were often mere apparitions, the spells of evil magicians in the Renaissance classics, so too the poet's vision vanishes in the first line of the first tercet as if it never were or ever could have been: "Oh, I know [my songs] are not worthy of such happiness." Again he is anxious that his sonnets might prove wearisome to his mistress. She should pity them, he concludes, for from them he has woven a wreath to cool his burning wounds and to provide something new for Slovenes. The last sonnet of the cycle ends in the bittersweet tone so beloved of European romantics in general. He has resigned himself again to his loveless fate, but he cannot refrain from imploring his mistress for mercy just one last time.

Prešeren's talent becomes manifest above all in the master sonnet, which follows the fourteenth and summarizes the cycle. Based on the mechanical transposition of each first line of the fourteen sonnets of the cycle, it not only makes sense—a feat in itself—but also expresses itself so naturally that we need not make any allowances for its origin. The master sonnet recapitulates the fate of

the "moist-flowering little roses of poetry" of the fourth sonnet,
which grow from the poet's heart as a monument to his love and a
novelty for the nation. In a general comparison the poet's heart then
becomes the country, surrounded by hostile forces, watered only
with tears, threatened with obliteration at its darkest hours. No
wonder the "little roses" are so pale. They need the rays from the
loved one's eyes in order to flower more gaily:

> Poet tvoj nov Slovencam venec vije,
> Ran mojih bo spomin in tvoje hvale,
> Iz srca svoje so kalí pognale
> Mokrócvetéče rož'ce poezije.
>
> Iz krajov niso, ki v njih sonce sije;
> Cel čas so blagih sapic pogrešvále,
> Obdajale so utrjene jih skale,
> Viharjov jeznih mrzle domačije.
>
> Izdíhljeji, solzé so jih redile,
> Jim moč so dale rasti nevesélo,
> Ur tèmnih so zatirale jih sile.
>
> Lej! torej je bledó njih cvetje velo,
> Jim iz oči tí pošlji žarke mile,
> In gnale bodo nov cvet bolj veselo.
>
> Your poet is weaving the Slovenes a new wreath,
> A monument to my wounds and to your praise.
> Forth from my heart have come to bud
> My poems' moist-flowering little roses.
>
> They are not from places where the sun shines;
> They have always lacked the soft winds,
> Above them have arisen rugged peaks,
> The chill homes of angry storms.
>
> Sighs and tears have nourished them,
> Gave them unhappy power to grow,
> The forces of dark hours have obliterated them.
>
> Look, that is why their blossoms are so pale.
> Send them the dear rays from your eyes.
> And they will bloom anew more joyously.

Of the three themes woven into the wreath, the erotic and the
patriotic receive little attention in the master sonnet. Only a couple

of lines and the implicit comparison of the poet's heart to the country remind us of the central issues of nine of the fourteen sonnets. It is the poetic theme which predominates. In part this arrangement is natural, for poetry was the specific concern of the last five sonnets of the wreath; the master sonnet merely continues that concern. But perhaps an even more important conclusion can be drawn from the evident bias toward the poetic in the fifteenth sonnet: it was not only the poet's last concern, but his chief one as well. In his poetry, Prešeren found peace (it "cools his stinging wounds," sonnet 14). Its rigid framework, its musicality, the certitude of its refrains and repetitions provided him with all the things his character craved but the world would not give him.[94] The vigor and precision of "A Wreath of Sonnets" reflect the extraordinary efforts the poet was still willing to undertake to achieve peace of mind: he still sought the world's approval and even more the reciprocation of his love for Julija.[95] The elevation of the poetic theme to the foremost of the three themes of the "Wreath" indicates, I believe, that the poet in the successful completion of this complex task he had set himself achieved some measure of inner peace. In transforming his frustrations into high poetry, he won relief from them, at least for a time.

C Individual Sonnets

In the period of his life immediately following the completion of the "Wreath," Prešeren continued to write sonnets. These were individual texts, however. He would never again undertake a sonnet cycle in Slovene after the completion of his masterpiece. Of those works written between 1834 and 1837, the year he composed his last Slovene sonnet,[96] he placed ten in his anthology after the "Wreath." Two written in that period he omitted; they were never published in his lifetime. Though not a cycle, these dozen sonnets all derive from a similar source, the sadness which darkened Prešeren's life during this time. Julija had definitively rejected the poet's suit, and later became engaged to his rival. His career was stalled with absolutely no prospects of revival. His closest relatives and dearest friend died. And his own health began to fail. These post-"Wreath" sonnets can be seen as a response to the ever-worsening circumstances of his personal life. They are also a poetic monument to the growing sophistication of Slovene literature of the 1830s at Prešeren's hand.

The first three sonnets of this part of the anthology plus a fourth not published there all have one thing in common. Prešeren wrote them on the borders of his copy of the "Wreath" as it was published in a separate edition of the *Illyrian List*.[97] Clearly they were intended as a coda to the "Wreath." Hence also their placement in the anthology following the cycle.

The first, "Ni znal molitve žlahtnič trde glave" [A nobleman with a hard head did not know any prayers, 1834], relates in the quatrains the legend of the nobleman who, short on intellect, could remember nothing except the beginning of the "Hail, Mary." But this he prayed faithfully, so much so that when he died a rose with those words on it in golden letters grew from his heart. This little tale becomes, in the concluding tercets,[98] an allegory of the "Wreath." The Virgin is Julija, "certainly no daughter of Eve" (i.e., divine, not human); the numbskull nobleman—Prešeren; and the constant prayer—the poet's impassioned courting. The rose, such a fitting comparison, represents the "Wreath," which springs from the poet's heart before death deprives him of his power. And the name in golden letters is, of course, the "Wreath's" acrostic.

This "epilogue" to the "Wreath" is obviously an apology. We know that the scandal following the publication of the poem and its acrostic caused Julija's mother to restrict further the already limited movements of her daughter.[99] The girl who had been forced to stay away from all frivolity for a year following her brother's death in 1832, was once again confined more or less to her home. She was allowed none of the social contacts normal for a girl of her age and station. It is hardly surprising then that she felt some antipathy toward the poet. Nor is it surprising to find him composing abject verse apologies to the girl he adored but from whom now he was even more distant. One might well wonder, though, how he expected her to react to these verses when she had so clearly misunderstood the compliment he had paid her in the "Wreath." Perhaps because he did not expect her to respond at all, Prešeren did not publish this sonnet or the following one until 1846.

The second sonnet, delightfully concise and pointed, begins "Sanjalo se mi je, de v svetem raji" [I dreamed that in the heavenly paradise, 1834]. The poet and his beloved have passed on to the next life, where they sit together in delirious joy. Petrarch and Laura are also there with them. The two women compare how they were praised during their earthly lives, while the two poets decide to measure their poems against one another on "St. Michael's scales." Of course Prešeren's are "lightweight" in comparison to those of the noble Italian, until the merits of Laura and Julija are also placed in the balance. Then Petrarch's side of the scale is no heavier than Prešeren's.

This sonnet of unabashed flattery has such a bright tone—in the sense of both musicality and light—that it forces us to realize anew how flexible a poet Prešeren could be in composing in whatever key he chose. The initial image, of paradise and the ultimate union of the poet and his mistress, predicts a happy resolution to his current misery, even if only "beyond the grave." (This note will sound again, quite forcefully, in "The Baptism on the Savica.") Of course, the point of the sonnet is to praise Julija's virtues, not to offer a poetic insight on the afterlife. Indeed, there is something inherently silly about an eternity where the immortals engage in such mundane actions as reading, weighing, or chatting. But precisely this silliness, of which the poet was no doubt quite conscious, contributes to the brightness of the depiction. The mild humor here is a welcome relief to the gloom of the other sonnets.

The clouds close in quickly again in the third and fourth sonnets, however: "Velíka, Togenburg, bila je mera" [Great, oh Toggenburg, was the measure of your patience, 1834)[100] and "Vi, ki vam je ljubezni tiranija" [You to whom love's tyranny is more unknown, 1834]. The first, borrowing a motif from Schiller, speaks of the impossibility of love for the poet in the here and now. He realizes, perhaps for the first time, that love is not going to play the role in his life that he had originally thought it might. The second sonnet would have been the last in the cycle if Prešeren had included it in the anthology. But in fact it was not printed until 1866. In its wrathful similes—the poet is as abused by love's tyranny as an American black by slavery, as oppressed by love as Balkan Christians are by Turks—the sonnet lashes out at those who despite all find some measure of contentment in life. The poet, unable to be happy, has begun to turn away from thoughts of love. In this poem at least he replaces them with thoughts of anger and disdain. Perhaps because these latter are out of keeping with the regretful tone of the cycle as a whole, however, Prešeren chose in the end to exclude this sonnet from the anthology.

Much more in keeping with the overall theme of apology, and therefore included in the *Poems*, is the sonnet "Bilo je, Mojzes! tebi naročeno" [It was given to you, Moses, 1834]. The poet draws a parallel between Moses's being called to lead the children of Israel to the promised land and the poet's being called to sing the loveliness and beauty of his mistress. Both men are absorbed totally in their function: both long to look at what has been promised to them. That alone is sufficient reward for all their suffering. The comparison is perhaps more telling than it at first seems to be. While Moses did indeed succeed in seeing the promised land, he was destined by God not to enter it. So too the poet dares to hope he might see his "promised land," but he realizes she will never be his. At last he has resigned himself to no more than a glance; that, he says, is "requital in full for the loneliness of piteous nights and days."

In 1836 Julija's engagement to Scheuchenstuel was made public. In response to that announcement, no doubt, Prešeren composed the following sonnet, "Na jasnem nebi mila luna sije" [In the bright sky the dear moon shines, 1837]. The conceit is quite Petrarchan. The moon shines, brightening everything and revealing the wonders of the night, but its light is not powerful enough to do any damage. Do not fear your poet's songs, Prešeren tells Julija. For the poet will continue to sing them until he dies. But without mutual love, their power is as reduced as that of the moon; while they will reveal his mistress' worth, in no way can they melt the ice of her heart. The calmer, resigned tone of this poem is due, most probably, to its late date of composition. The neatness of its construction, the enumeration in line 10 ("Your poet, you, your fiancé, your mother!"), give the work an almost detached and reflective air. And of course the image of the moon sheds cool light on the poem, while the poet eschews any ardor that might be connected with the sun. This sonnet completes the first half of the ten poems which follow the "Wreath"; it also signals, perhaps, the extinction of the last fires the poet had kept burning for his beloved for so long.

A familiar feature occurs in the sonnet "Marskteri romar gre v Rim, v Kompostelje" [Many a pilgrim goes to Rome, to Compostela, 1834],[101] an acrostic. The poet dedicated this work to Matevž Langus, the noted Ljubljana artist, because he had painted Julija's portrait: the first letter of each line spells out "Matevžu Langusu" ("To Matevž Langus"). Just as pilgrims go to the shrines of Christendom, says the poet, to glimpse a view of heavenly glory and to cool their desires in the presence of Godly love, so the poet visits his friend's studio to see the portrait of his beloved which hangs there. False dreams and overpowering desire drive him to it, where despair is less painful, time shorter, and sighs more profound.

Contemplation replaces the poet's courting and even his despair.

The religious imagery, with its leitmotiv of a more glorious life after death, serves as a vehicle for introducing the rationale of the poet's new activity. He makes it quite clear, however, that his deity is not the Christian God, but his beloved. A great sadness is implicit, therefore, in this sonnet: his "goddess" offers no afterlife where justice and love will triumph. All his contemplation of her can net him is perhaps a shorter life ("the shorter flow of time") and less pain. She is, in effect, a goddess of death, to whom he sacrifices the sad remnants of his life.

In the final sonnet of the group, "Odprlo bo nebo po sodnem dnevi" [Heaven will open on judgment day, 1837],[102] the lover persona of the poet at last does indeed die. He compares himself to the damned, whose misery on the last day will be even greater in contrast to the joy of the elect. His joy once had been ineffable, when his beloved had smiled on him. But now that glance, ever before him, drives him along the infinite road to the pit of despair.

This last sonnet represents Prešeren's most mature and most profound expression of grief at the unhappy resolution of his "affair" with Julija Primic. Among the last he ever wrote, it terminates an era for him, as well as closing this section of the anthology. The riven poet, who in contrasts of happiness with misery has constructed powerful images of his own internal sundering, finally gives up. The note struck in the last sonnet is one of finality—he cannot bear any longer to speak his grief out loud. Rather even he must move out of the realm of words and rhymes: not coincidentally "nezrečena" ("ineffable") is used twice in this last sonnet, and, uniquely in all of Prešeren's poems, the rhyme scheme has been condensed to a bare minimum, a b b a a b b a b c b c b c. The poetic persona of Julija dies here, together with the persona of the poet who so steadfastly sought her. Neither will ever be heard from again.

D *"Humorous Sonnets"*

Perhaps as a relief from the gloom of the preceding sonnets, certainly as a further demonstration of the possibilities of the sonnet form, Prešeren continued his anthology with a cycle he called "Zabavljivi sonetje" [Humorous Sonnets]. The name is not quite appropriate, however. Unlike other of Prešeren's poems, which are gently humorous, these three sonnets (plus a fourth not published in the anthology but clearly similar to those that were) are heavily ironic, in the best tradition of antique satirists. Each is directed both

at a specific cultural figure of Prešeren's day and at the issue he
represented. Each by implication gives Prešeren's view on Slovene
literary and cultural life. The poems must, therefore, be considered
not only as poetic but also political texts.

The target of the first sonnet, "Al prav se piše kaша ili kaʃha?"
[Is it correct to write 'kaша' or 'kaʃha', 1831] is Franc Metelko and
his newly developed alphabet. Is it better to write "kasha" (boiled
groats, a favorite dish of many Eastern Europeans) with one of the
new letters (ш) or with the old digraph of the "bohoričica" (ʃh)?
Unless one or the other makes the kasha taste better, Prešeren says,
then most Slovenes would agree arguing about it as sensible as
calculating the damage done by a donkey's shadow.

When the poem was printed in 1832, it contributed enormously
to the Ljubljana ABC War, for its personal attacks (Prešeren, for
example, calls Kopitar "the old hoof" ["kopito" in Slovene]) added
insult to the injury Čop was about to do to the "metelčica" in
having it banned. But while its immediate effect may have been to
exacerbate matters, over the long run it certainly served to point up
the silliness of arguing over spelling when the language still had so
little written in it. The sonnet attempted to show the cart was before
the horse; Prešeren's other work attempted to put the horse up front
again.

The second sonnet, "Ne bod'mo šalobarde! Moskvičanov" [Let's
not be fools! The Muscovites' books, 1831], is directed against Jakob
Zupan, a Jansenist contributor to the *Carniolan Bee*, who with
others sought to expand the Slovene literary language by borrowing
useful words from the other Slavs.[103] Slavization, as it is called,[104]
was both necessary and successful in Slovene: the modern literary
language is indebted both for words and forms to other Slavic
languages. Prešeren's point in his sonnet was not aimed, however,
at the process so much as the distortion of the process through
excessive borrowing. Sarcastically he advises his fellow Upper
Carniolans, whose dialect was the basis for the literary language of
the time, to pick up all the pleasing words from Muscovite books
and bring them home, like crows building a bigger nest. Thus they
would through "stealing" enrich the new language of the "Slovene
Illyrians." If the process goes on long enough, he says, then the
oldest Slavic language (according to Kopitar's view of Slovene)[105]
will become just like what the Babylonians spoke after God confused
their tongues.

The indirect reference to one of Kopitar's ideas in the second

"Humorous Sonnet" gives us another insight into the fruitful intellectual relationship the poet enjoyed with the linguist. But their social-political relationship was anything but cordial, as the third sonnet, "Apel podobo na ogled postavi" [Apelles puts a picture on display, 1831], clearly shows. Its target is even named in the last line of the sonnet: Kopitar. Borrowing once again from classical antiquity for his plot, Prešeren tells of the famous artist Apelles, who displayed a picture, then hid behind it to hear the comments of the passers-by. A blacksmith disliked the proportions of the hooves; respecting the opinion of this "expert," Apelles corrected his painting. But when the same smith returned the next day and started to criticize the figures' calves, Apelles drove him away. Addressing this "overstuffed carper," Prešeren quotes the proverb: "The cobbler should stick to his last." The word "cobbler" in Slovene is *kopitar*, and Prešeren chose to spell it with a capital *K*.

Prešeren disliked intensely Kopitar's interference as a would-be critic of his poems. He felt, with ample justification, that Kopitar had little competence in judging poetic texts.[106] And even if he were a careful reader, his biases in favor of the pious and the peasant automatically turned him against Prešeren's romantic works. In effect Prešeren told the Slovene linguist and censor to mind his own linguistic business.

E   *The "Sonnets of Unhappiness"*

Originally there were seven "Sonetje nesreče" [Sonnets of Unhappiness, 1832], but Prešeren published only six of them in his lifetime. One poem in the cycle, "Pov'do let starih čudne izročila" [Wonderous tales of ancient years are told] did not appear in print until 1909. Judging from Prešeren's manuscript, we know he meant this sonnet to be first.[107] Why he dropped it remains a mystery, although at least one convincing explanation has been suggested. In our treatment here, we consider it in its original position, as the opening work of the cycle.

Taken all together, the "Sonnets of Unhappiness" are perhaps the grimmest of Prešeren's poems. Coming as they do as the last sonnet cycle of his anthology, although they predate the "Wreath" and all the individual sonnets, they represent the "last word" in Prešeren's expressions of love and disappointment in the sonnet form. Their theme is more global than in many of the other sonnets: life itself has been examined and found not merely wanting, but absurd and destructive. The "I" of the first, second, and seventh sonnets (which frame the cycle whether it is taken in its original version or that of 1846) rejects both faith and suicide as possible means of handling life. Only resignation remains. In essence resignation is for the poet a recognition of the absurdity of life and a decision to accept all life's blows. The poet is completely beaten by the end of the cycle. The utter hopelessness of his situation exceeds that portrayed in any other poetry Prešeren wrote.

Were he to have stayed with his original scheme, this most despairing of cycles would have been opened with a bizarre sonnet drawing on the vampire legend.[108] The poem speaks of jilted women who haunt their faithless lovers after death. They can be satisfied, momentarily, by drinking their lovers' blood. So, too, the poet is pursued by his own Fury. His muse has been driven off by this goddess of the dead, "whose song is a curse." She never ceases to consume the poet's happiness.

Slodnjak has conceived an interesting theory concerning Prešeren's reason for suppressing this sonnet: it was too autobiographical.[109] He hypothesizes that it may have been written as an act of contrition when the poet learned of the death of Maria Khlun, the German woman from Graz whom for a while he intended to marry. Since Khlun's date of death is unknown, this theory obviously rests on circumstantial evidence alone. But the poet's conscience may have been plagued if he felt his rejection of Khlun had contributed to her death, or at least to her great unhappiness.[110] The sonnet seems to speak of the poet's uneasy conscience concerning an affair in which he was the unfaithful partner. If the connection with Khlun and Slodnjak's theory is valid, then Prešeren may have dropped this first sonnet to save himself any further embarrassment from the affair.

On the other hand, the suppression may also have occurred for poetic reasons. "Marvelous tales" does not really belong in the cycle, for it undermines the poet's pose as the hapless victim of fate's blows. For once, the poet causes his own unhappiness. He is not quite the innocent plaything of fate he portrays himself to be in all the other sonnets. Perhaps he felt that contradiction himself, and decided to eliminate it by removing the poem. Unfortunately, in so doing he excluded a rather unique expression of poetic remorse from his printed canon. But he did restore unity to his cycle.

The second sonnet, "O Vrba! Srečna, draga vas domača" [Oh Vrba! Happy, dear home village], explicitly autobiographical, is also strangely idyllic, thanks to the frequent use in the verses of the conditional mood. The poet laments having left his father's home for the world, in order to slake his thirst for knowledge. He never would have known frustration or "inner storms." He would have wed a faithful, hardworking village girl, his "ship" would have sailed life's sea smoothly, and his "neighbor," St. Mark, the patron of the parish church in Vrba, would have guarded him and his family from all evil.

The sadness of this sonnet cannot be gainsaid. As in other poems of his, Prešeren makes his point by contrast between reality and his idealized world. The quatrains, full of bitterness, depict reality; acquisitiveness, dissatisfaction, deception, frustration, disappointment, victimization. The tercets offer a glimpse of the poet's ideal: faithfulness in love, simplicity, serenity, perhaps even religious faith. The poet has been driven out of this Eden by his curiosity. The world he is forced to inhabit is made even sadder by that vision of abandoned happiness that could have been his.

Unlike the first sonnet, whose biographical tone pointed up the poet's complicity in his own unhappiness, the second sonnet excuses him from complicity by making his sin the sin of Adam and Eve. If partaking of the fruit of the tree of knowledge proved irresistible for demigods, how much more so was it for the simple village boy? Thus, we infer, he is not to be blamed for what is, in effect, a flaw in the creation. The second sonnet launches the idea of the poet as a victim who, whatever his shortcomings, does not deserve what fate has done to him.

The next two sonnets avoid autobiography, while they build upon the initial image of the poet's own sadness. "Popotnik pride v Afrike pušavo" [A traveler comes to Africa's desert] tells of one who wanders in the dark, wishing for light. When the moon shines through the clouds, however, the wanderer realizes, as he never had before, in what dire peril he finds himself. He resembles the youth for whom the future is unknown. He is driven to learn about it but when he does a loathing for life afflicts him, and an abyss looms before him without one safe path. We are not told specifically what has driven Prešeren to this realization about the bleakness of his future. We are only allowed to share his angst as he contemplates it.

The fourth sonnet, "Hrast, ki vihar na tla ga zimski tresne" [The oak, which a winter storm strikes to the ground], allegorizes hope in the form of a tree which, even though knocked down, still sends forth a few last sprigs in spring, until rot completely kills it. This hope is the candle of life, the poet says. From day to day it gutters more until it goes out for lack of proper care. Hope therefore is the essential sign of life. Despite the attacks of "inimical fortune," it tries to endure, but inevitably it is snuffed out, for there is nothing in the world to nurture hope. The poem concludes that extinguishing hope is tantamount to the ending of life.

The fifth sonnet, "Komur je sreče dar bila klofuta" [For him to whom fate's gift was a slap], continues the exploration from the preceding sonnet of the encounter between life and fate. Even were one a giant, fate would overwhelm him. There is no country where one can take refuge from sorrow and need, except the grave. The last tercet speaks lovingly of the respite that death brings to those who suffer. After completely avoiding it for two sonnets, Prešeren very gingerly reintroduces an autobiographical note here. Like me, he says, those who have offended fate have no chance for salvation. But the sonnet is still largely descriptive. Its conclusion, that death appears to be the only resolution for life's problems, is kept safely insulated from the single first person reference at the beginning of the poem.

This fifth sonnet is closely linked to the second in the cycle. The poet, cast from his Eden, is searching for a country and a home he can call his own. But he finds none. Everywhere the frustrations of life outside Eden surround him. Only one thing attracts him, and that is the very thing with which mankind was cursed after the expulsion: death. In mortality he sees the only way to return to the serenity he so dreamed of in his native village. Yet he is not quite ready here fully to embrace relief-giving death.

Sonnet 6, "Življenje ječa, čas v nji rabelj hudi" [Life is a prison, time the evil hangman in it], is without doubt Prešeren's greatest celebration of death, and perhaps one of the finest in South Slavic literature. Once again the poet begins to speak, though somewhat warily, of himself. He appears in the closest association with death, which is "the key, the door, the happy path, / Which leads us from the city of pain." Where death brings us is explained in an anaphora covering five lines, each beginning "where." Death is the deliverance from the jail of life. It brings us to a place where rust breaks all chains, persecutors cannot follow us, where injustices cease, men lose their burdens. It leads us to the deepest sleep which care's loudest noises cannot disturb.

Again Prešeren works the contrast between reality and the ideal. He seems on the point of embracing death as his answer to a life he can no longer stand. His ideal has now become rest. Respite from

care is the only thing he seeks, unlike that earlier time when he
actually dared to desire faithfulness, serenity, love, and so on. But
though peace would come in death, in this sonnet he is still very
wary of accepting death—presumably in the form of suicide—as *his*
way out. He carefully keeps to the plural "we" as he describes the
benefits of suicide. In terms of the cycle this distinction is critical,
for it brings the poet to the last sonnet, where, as in the first two, he
once again speaks fully from and of himself alone.

In the seventh sonnet, "Čez tebe več ne bo, sovražna sreča!"
[Through you shall no more come, inimical fortune!] the poet finally
gives his credo. Life, though not worth living, must be borne.
Complaining must cease, one must become accustomed to enduring; the body must grow tough, and the spirit numbed. As in the
epigraph to the anthology, fear and hope have once again abandoned the poet. Now, he says, if fate caresses or beats him, it will
find him "an unfeeling block."

Thus the poet winds up advocating a death of a different kind
than the physical elimination of the person. Rather he seeks to
extinguish that part of him that is most sensitive, that reacts
(especially with words) to the misery within him. The poet wants
release from his poetic self. That is the only way, he says, he will be
able to tolerate life. His "too lively heart" must turn to stone.

Small wonder, then, that Prešeren placed the "Sonnets of Unhappiness" at the end of his anthology. Especially the six printed in
Poems form together an exquisite statement of the poet's sufferings
as a poet. He found no release in his poetry, so he tells us here, but
rather an exacerbation of his grief and misery through the sharpen-
ing of his senses which poetry not only required from him but
produced in him as well. If we consider their place in Prešeren's
biography, the "Sonnets of Unhappiness" read almost like a predic-
tion of the misery that would befall the poet in his hopeless, fervent
courting of Julija. Especially in that relationship we have a sense
that his erotic drives were not diminished by his poetry, but rather
fed. Fortunately for ensuing generations the poet did not heed his
own advice, given in the "Sonnets of Unhappiness," to eliminate
his poetic feelings. Quite the contrary; he realized that only one
attitude was possible for him in life: to bear it "without peace."
That is, he could not make himself into an insensitive block, nor
could he kill himself, nor could he make himself happy. Therefore
his only recourse was to accept all the tensions and somehow
endure. Resignation in the face of all life's frustrations, repression of

all his instincts, finally became the poet's resolution to the absurdity he found life to be.

The last poem of the section really does not belong to the sonnet section at all. It is "Matiju Čopu" [To Matija Čop, 1835] and in fact it is the dedication to "The Baptism on the Savica," which follows it immediately (the two were published together in 1836). By form, however, it is a sonnet, and Prešeren must have considered its placement here a useful bridge between not only two sections of his book, but the two major parts of his oeuvre also, his sonnets and his epic poem. Furthermore, it stresses by virtue of its position the central role the poet always felt Čop had played in his creativity. For Čop was one of the major forces in encouraging Prešeren to try the sonnet form, and it was in memory of his deceased friend that Prešeren composed the "Baptism."

Of the five poems Prešeren wrote for his friend, this one tells us the least about him. Indeed, were it not for the title it would be almost impossible to guess which one of Prešeren's several deceased friends the poet had in mind. What the sonnet, with its Petrarchan tercet rhyme scheme, does tell us is the idea of what is to follow. Happiness, he declares, is possible only beyond the grave; this life has nothing to offer. It is best to refrain from "high-flying thoughts" and desire, to give up all hope of happiness on earth. Death with its restfulness will soon claim both the happy and the pained heart. The very final sonnet, then, of the longest and most important section of Prešeren's poetic anthology is a call, once again, to resignation. It sums up not only the poet's experience with life and love, but also the vast majority of his poems as well. Of all the poet's postures, this one corresponds perhaps most closely to his own private view of life. Although in many senses he did not resign himself to the kind of indifference he promoted, nevertheless he remained true to the ideal of resignation in everything he wrote. We get further confirmation of that viewpoint in "The Baptism on the Savica."

VII   "*The Baptism on the Savica*"

Prešeren published his longest work, "Krst pri Savici" [The Baptism on the Savica, 1835] in April 1836, in a run of 600 copies printed on special paper in order, as he himself wrote, "to have at least that advantage over other Carniolan writers."[111] This unique work of Slovene literature he asked to be considered as a "metrical exercise," which he had composed merely to "gain the good graces

of the clergy," who in the final analysis seemed to be pleased with
it and him. Typical of his sense of humor, the poet added: "It would
give me greater pleasure, however, if they bought my poetry rather
than just praised it."[112]

The importance of the work in his corpus, and in the whole body
of Slovene literature in general, belies the jocular tone of Prešeren's
comments about his "Baptism." The poet himself thought enough
of his "exercise" to have it republished in the Peasants' and Artisans'
News in 1844, and then to place it at the end of his 1846 anthology
where, according to one critic, it serves as the "focus" of the entire
collection.[113] Over the years the opinions of other critics have varied
concerning the merits of the "Baptism" relative to Prešeren's other
poetry. Estimations in fact run from mild disappointment with the
epic to an enthusiastic acceptance of it as Prešeren's "most mature
work."[114] But by and large the verdict of critics and readers has
been delivered: the "Baptism" occupies a unique and outstanding
place in Slovene, for not only was it the first major work of the
infant literature but it also gave expression to a national awareness
which before it had been shared by only a few. As a work of patriotic
poetry it has been an unqualified success.

Critics, however, have been especially vexed by certain considerations that have to do with the "Baptism" as pure poetry or as
"Gedankenspoesie" ("reflective poetry"). The problems seem to be
basically three: How original is the epic? What role does religion
play in it? What does it mean? When we consider the variety of
sources which Prešeren is alleged to have drawn on to write the
"Baptism"—the Bible, Homer, St. Augustine, Dante, Petrarch,
Tasso,[115] Chateaubriand, the Schlegel brothers, Ernst Schulze,
Alexander von Starnberg-Ungern, David Strauss, Jan Kollár, and
Adam Mickiewicz comprise a partial list—then the problem of
originality seems overwhelming and almost insoluble. But the poet
himself sought to allay misgivings about the sources of his poem by
citing the work from which he drew his historical facts, the Slovene
historian Janez Vajkart Valvasor's The Honor of the Duchy of
Carniola (1689).[116] As for his artistic sources, Slodnjak has sliced
neatly through that Gordian knot by saying that in the final analysis
questions of originality are irrelevant.[117] The epic genre makes
ample provision for the use of earlier models, and originality in it
should be gauged not by the novelty of the imagery and expression
so much as the success with which borrowings and innovations are
woven together to form a coherent whole. In this light one would be

hard pressed to deny the very profound originality of the "Baptism" which, drawing motifs from the most diverse sources, successfully integrates them into a unified, unique literary expression.

A more embarrassing issue, particularly for contemporary critics of Prešeren's "Baptism," is its religious setting. In analyzing the poem, many critics feel called upon to dismiss any direct religious intention on the part of the poet.[118] They prefer instead to read the religious points of the poem as allegories of Prešeren's own world view, which was noncomittal. In this way they gain support both from the sarcastic tone of the poet's own comment on the poem, that he wrote it to "please the clerics," and from his well-known "Freigeisterei" ("free-spiritedness"). Their embarrassment stems, of course, from having to take seriously the poet's cynical comments about using religion for such ignoble purposes.

An objective reader can hardly construe the "Baptism" as a defense of Christianity or of Catholic dogma. The hero, Črtomir, asks enough penetrating questions, and his conversion is halfhearted enough, to leave the most devout believer with misgivings about the forced Christianization of the Slovene lands in the eighth century. But it would be an equal distortion of the text to ignore the profundity or authenticity of Bogomila's conversion, as the poet carefully elaborates it in eleven and a half stanzas (24-35).[119] Nor would it do to underestimate the importance of the priest in answering Črtomir's probing questions,[120] nor finally the role of St. Augustine's *City of God*, which Prešeren himself mentions in connection with the "Baptism"[121] as a source of his views. The religious material in the "Baptism" is all *ancillary*, however, to the main line of the poem, which is the struggle of Črtomir to find happiness in the world. It provides the atmosphere, the structure, but not the heart of the poem.

Before we approach the third issue with which the critics have most often concerned themselves in analyzing the "Baptism"—its meaning—we should turn to the poem itself, for to most non-Slovenes its contents are unfamiliar. This work is the very late flowering of a genre that began in Europe with Homer. By the time Prešeren composed it, the epic impulse in Western European countries had turned to prose forms, especially the novel and the drama, to record the larger issues of social life and thought. We cannot know what ultimately prompted Prešeren to compose an epic poem. He may not have regarded prose composition as one of his strengths. Or he may have wanted to give his nation a national

epic, even a belated one, so that Slovenes could boast of the same
sorts of literary masterpieces that Poles and Czechs and Russians,
not to mention Western Europeans, possessed in their national
literatures. Or, in answer to the question he posed to Čop in 1832[122]
about the characteristics of a romantic tragedy for Slovene, he may
have received advice to try his hand at an epic instead. In any event,
when he sat down to write the "Baptism" after the death of his
friend in 1835, he took an epic approach to his materials, with,
however, a powerful dramatic influence visible especially toward
the end of the work.

In all, the "Baptism on the Savica," including the sonnet to Čop,
consists of 525 iambic pentameters. The first fourteen are, as we
have seen, in sonnet form. The second group, of seventy-nine, are
arranged in twenty-six tercets, with the last tercet having an extra
line to complete the terza rima that unites them all. The largest
section, the "Baptism" itself, is composed of fifty-four eight-line
stanzas (there were only fifty-three in the edition of 1836), arranged
in standard ottava rima: *a b a b a b c c*. Prešeren had no humorous
intent in his selection of this verse form, although historically ottava
rima has been associated in lengthy narratives with the comic
masterpieces (Boccaccio, Ariosto, Byron).[123] Perhaps his appreciation of the serious possibilities of ottava rima should be traced to
Torquato Tasso, who used it so effectively in his epic *Jerusalem
Liberated* (1575).

From the beginning the reader is impressed by a certain looseness
among the parts of the "Baptism." The dedicational sonnet, for
example, really stands apart from the text of the poem itself. In fact,
the poet dropped it from the edition published in 1844, but
reinstated it in 1846.[124] The other two parts, as a result of the
difference between terza and ottava rima, appear and read quite
differently. The scope of the introduction is broad and epic in
action, information, details, and coloring. The "Baptism" proper
has a much narrower range, focusing exclusively on Črtomir, who
the whole while stands on the shores of Lake Bohinj, in northwestern
Slovenia. What ties these three disparate parts together is only
Črtomir. He alone is mentioned in each, and it is the elaboration of
his problems which moves the reader through the poem.

At the very outset, in the sonnet, Prešeren identifies himself with
Črtomir: "High-flying thoughts I have buried, / The pains of
unfulfilled desires, / Like Črtomir, all hope of happiness on earth."
In the introduction the reader is told who Črtomir is: the youngest,

and last Slovene pagan still holding out against the forced Christianization of his people by the Germans. With most of the country
converted and Slovene now fighting Slovene over the religious issue,
Črtomir and his remaining loyal troops flee to a fortress on Lake
Bohinj to make a final stand. His enemies besiege the place, and as
the food supply dwindles Črtomir decides on a desperate step: he
and his men will steal out of the fort under cover of night in the
hope of avoiding a final showdown with the numerically superior
Christian forces. In a speech to his men he says:

> 16. More of the world belongs to Slava's children,
>   We will find a way to that place where her sons
>   Choose as free men their faith and ways.

> 17. And if the gods give us up to death,
>   The night in earth's dark bosom is less terrifying
>   Than enslaved days under the bright sun!

Unfortunately the Christians surprise the pagans just as they are
leaving their fortress. In the ensuing battle, all the non-Christians
are killed and half the Christians. Only Črtomir of all his army
somehow escapes.

Črtomir is the classical hero, brave, wise, and good. And the
pattern of the introduction is equally classical—historical, dramatic,
brief, symbolic—along the lines that the Schlegels had set up for an
epic. The principal departure from their program lies in Črtomir's
paganism: rather than an apologist for Christianity, as the Schlegels
had suggested a proper epic hero be, Prešeren has created an
attractive anti-Christian, and chosen to identify Christianity with
the enemies of his nation.[125] In this departure lies very much the
meaning of Črtomir in this part of the poem. He represents the
nation. His respect for its religion is based merely on his love for the
tradition it implies—to religion as such he is indifferent.[126] His real
battle is not against Christianity per se, but against the imposition
by force of an alien doctrine. He is at once freedom fighter,
traditionalist, and national particularist. He opposes the enslavers
who would impose a faith that was international. He wants his own,
such as it is. He stands for Slovene apartness. From the very
beginning he is clearly doomed.

The possibilities for extended expression offered by the larger
verse units of the "Baptism" proper allowed the poet to delve into

the inner workings of his hero's mind. Now no longer a national leader, Črtomir stands wretched and alone, contemplating suicide on the shore of Bohinj. Immediately the poet reestablishes the link between himself and his hero: he says he knows how the defeated man feels, and also what alone keeps him from killing himself.[127] He speaks of the storms in Črtomir's breast, and of the love the young pagan shared with Bogomila, the priestess of Živa, the Slavic goddess of love. In a flashback the poet recalls (stanzas 6-14) their love and their final separation, as Črtomir went off to fight. The memory so disturbs Črtomir that he moves to take his life: (15) "But something stops his over anxious hand—/ It was, Bogomila, your beautiful / Image, which had earlier delivered him from the battle."

He decides to see her again, if she is still alive. At that juncture a fisherman arrives and ferries him to the Savica waterfall, at the other end of the lake, to keep him safe overnight from the Christians and to help him as best he can. The fisherman goes off to fetch Bogomila. At daybreak the man returns. With him are Bogomila and—a Christian priest.

Up to this point the "Baptism" is pure narrative: even the dialogue between Črtomir and the fisherman is given in the third person. Then the presentation abruptly changes. From stanza 23 to 49 dialogue alone is used to report the thoughts and feelings of the characters. Only three people speak: Bogomila, who has the lion's share of these stanzas (seventeen and a half), Črtomir, who speaks in six, and the priest, who speaks in three. Until the last stanza of the complete poem (54) the action takes place at the Savica waterfall; the time elapsed certainly does not encompass more than a morning. Thus the latter part of the "Baptism" observes all the classical unities of the drama (time, place, and action).

Not only the structure, but the content of this latter half is dramatic as well. Prešeren brings face to face his two principals, Črtomir, the desperate, pursued, suicidal pagan, and Bogomila, the woman he loves but no longer really knows. In his absence she has changed. She has rejected the pagan faith of their people, and along with her father, who also used to serve the goddess Živa, she has been baptized a Christian. In the longest speech in the poem (eleven and a half stanzas) she explains why she has converted: after Črtomir's departure she was tortured by thoughts of the danger he was in; furthermore, if he died, their love would die with him. At this vulnerable moment she heard a priest preaching to the people in the marketplace. In her retelling of his tale of creation and salvation it is evident he struck all the most responsive chords in her: about original sin, the salvation God's Son offers to all nations, that God is the God of love, that earth is merely preparatory to the everlasting joy of heaven, that in heaven all who love here are joined together forever.

The priest singles her out after his sermon, and she brings him home for further instruction. There he repeats in shorter form his catechism and baptizes father and daughter. Her mind then turns again to thoughts of Črtomir: what if he should die outside the state of grace? The priest advises prayer. She implores God to save him. To her prayers she ascribes his safety that night when all the other pagans were slaughtered at the beseiged fortress.

Črtomir, evidently moved by her continued love for him, says that he is willing to do anything she asks. But how can she forget the evil the Christians have done to their people in the name of this "God of love"? At this point the priest answers Črtomir's objections with orthodox Christianity. He says Christianity is a faith of brotherhood and equality of all peoples, a faith of love for all. Črtomir's enemies, on the other hand, are not doing God's work, but advancing only their own. In effect they do not represent Christ, though they fight under a Christian banner. This answer apparently satisfies Črtomir, for he accepts *Bogomila*'s faith (obviously only because it is hers) and rejects the pagan beliefs of his nation. When, he asks her, will both baptism *and* marriage unite the two of them?

The climax of the dialogue occurs in the next five stanzas (40-44). Bogomila explains that life on this earth is short, especially in comparison to the eternity of heaven. Mindful that their momentary union here might endanger their eternal residence together in paradise, she has vowed chastity before God and the Blessed Virgin. To save him from death and help him get to heaven, she has renounced all possibility of an earthly marriage. She has become Christ's bride. To this the priest adds that Črtomir may not marry either, for to offer reparation for the misery he has caused in defending his false faith, he is to become a priest and hence celibate himself. Renouncing also all hope of earthly happiness, he must help convert his nation to the true faith.

Črtomir does not understand the priest, but he has heard Bogomila. He laments that happiness never was meant to be his on earth, that once their love had made him joyous, but it was very short-lived. Now, he says, everything has been lost: "Flight is my hope, the forest my home for now. / Union would be unwise with me /

Whom angry fate eternally pursues" (46). Bogomila corrects him, however: he must not think that she does not love him, although they cannot marry. Her love cannot be snuffed out by angry fate; on the contrary it will be purer and more faithful for its renunciation here. It will be better in heaven. Then she reiterates the priest's charge to him, to go preach the Gospel in Slovene towns.

As she tells him this, a rainbow appears and shines on Bogomila. This ancient indication of God's favor overwhelms Črtomir. He is enthralled by her glorification. He then accepts the charge she and the priest have given him, gives away all his fortune (which Bogomila's father has been holding for him), and bids his beloved a chaste good-bye. But before he goes off, Bogomila asks for one more favor: that he be baptized there in her presence. She wants to rest assured that in the dangers he is about to face his soul at least will be safe. "Silently Črtomir accedes to that request," says the poet returning in the last two stanzas to the narrative mode. He and the priest pray, while the face of the girl who once was Živa's handmaiden becomes "radiant with joy." In the fifty-fourth and final stanza the poet completes his tale in a few brief strokes: Črtomir is ordained at Aquileia and preaches the Gospel to the Slovenes and even beyond their borders until his death; Bogomila returns home with her father: She and Črtomir "never see each other again in this world."

The problem of the meaning of the "Baptism on the Savica" (to return to the third, and most difficult issue addressed by all of Prešeren's critics) continues to be the liveliest of all the areas of interest in the poem today. After so many generations and so many interpretations, obviously we are faced with not one, but plural meanings of the work. These differ not only in kind, that is, a philosophical meaning, a poetic meaning, or a national-political meaning, but within one kind as well, so that one critic may see the poem as the philosophical exploration of the erotic,[128] while another construes it as an answer to the poet's suicidal impulses.[129]

Perhaps the simplest way to approach the meaning of the "Baptism" is as an allegory of Prešeren's own life. The poet makes it quite clear from the beginning that he identifies closely with Črtomir. The erotic misadventures of the pagan parallel closely— though of course not exactly—the poet's own experiences. And Bogomila's resistance to his advances reads like Julija's rejection of Prešeren's suit, albeit in an idealized way which imputes to her far nobler motives than Julija had in real life. Črtomir's failure at war then becomes Prešeren's professional troubles. The isolation of the one is the loneliness of the other after the death of all his comrades. And the priest is an allegorization of Prešeren's own conscience which, at the poet's most troubled moments, reminds him of his duty to himself (to stay alive) and his people (to spread the "Gospel" of poetry). The conclusion of the poem is very much in keeping with the conclusions reached in so many other of Prešeren's poems: that the only way to deal with the absurdities of this world is to resign oneself to them, and to renounce all thought of an earthly joy derived from one's own righteousness or the justice of one's cause. In the end Črtomir accepts all the penance laid on him by the priest and Bogomila, even though his conversion to their faith is halfhearted at best. His conversion is equivalent in the poet's life to the realization that one sometimes must do things (like living and writing) without either knowing why or really wanting to.

But the "Baptism" need not be read only on a personal level, as an allegory of Prešeren's own life, however much such a reading may help us to understand the mournful tone of the poem. We can also appreciate it on a national-cultural level, as an epic statement about the fate of the Slovenes. If we choose to read it thus, then we soon perceive the tragedy of the nation as Prešeren saw it. However much we may side with Črtomir and his band of patriots, and however much we may detest the bloody, rapacious ways of the foreign crusaders, the fact nonetheless remains that Črtomir was resisting an important advancement for his nation. By fighting Christianity he sought to keep the Slovenes out of the ethical and cultural community of Central European and Mediterranean Christianity. Without the civilizing impulses from there, the nation would surely have retreated further into barbarism, and eventually been extirpated.

Of course in the introduction Črtomir is resisting foreign enslavement as well. But it becomes evident that his general resistance is wrongheaded when, in the "Baptism" proper, he is nonetheless "forced" into conversion by Bogomila, who with the priest represents true Christianity. The lesson still stands then: the nation must be compelled to accept the better way, despite what compulsion may entail in suffering and sacrifice. For without the change no future is possible; with it at least some possibility exists for continued existence as an ethnic entity. And if some of the very traditions which provided the cohesiveness of that entity must be renounced, then it is up to those who survive the changes to adopt the new

forms to their own ends, and make them into new traditions binding
once again all the people into one national unit. That, for example,
is why Črtomir has to become a priest. It would not have sufficed
for him merely to have accepted the new faith and renounced the
old. He had to make the new faith into a new national expression, if
his conversion were to make any sense at all.

What lessons Prešeren may have thought to draw from his epic to
apply to the national-cultural scene in his day we may only guess.
But behind this eighth-century allegory a point is likely being made.
Once again in Prešeren's time the nation was faced with the
necessary but painful acceptance of foreign influence, this time in
the cultural field. Prešeren and Čop recognized the necessity of
adopting the new European romantic forms, which so many other
Slovenes—Kopitar, for example—wanted to shun. Without input
from abroad, in terms of forms, motifs, ideas, a modern Slovene
literature would never have been born. And if the nation were
excluded from the cultural community of Europe in the nineteenth
century, then, just as surely as if it had been excluded from the
religious community of the eighth century, it would eventually die
out. On a national-cultural level the "Baptism" can be interpreted
as the poet's warning to his fellow countrymen that the fate of their
small nation lay with learning to accept the inevitable, and often
superior, impositions of the larger European community and to
adopt them for profitable local use as tools to maintain the nation.

A level of poetic meaning inheres as well in the "Baptism." This
epic is Prešeren's last attempt, as far as we know,[130] to synthesize so
many of his views in a genre till then totally new to Slovene. Though
he wrote many brilliant poems after the "Baptism," this epic was
his last genuine tour de force. After 1836 a physical and emotional
disintegration set in which inhibited his ever undertaking such a
large-scale project again. The movement from the epic to the
dramatic in the "Baptism" itself may signal an early stage in his
growing ambivalence toward his own poetry. The failure to sustain
an epic perspective throughout the poem, even his selection of the
somewhat old-fashioned epic genre to begin with, betray an artistic
uncertainty which was lacking in the poet just a few years before,
when Čop was still alive.

The poetic point of the "Baptism" is that it is Prešeren's last
attempt to incorporate into Slovene a new form of European poetry.
Unfortunately he did not quite bring it off. The resulting product,
while unique and engaging, was still, in the poet's own words, a

"metrical exercise." Without Čop, who had been not only his intermediary to other European literatures, but their interpreter and the poet's first and most sophisticated critic, Prešeren could not make the necessary adaptations. More than a testimony to their friendship, the "Baptism" is a monument to the collaboration of Prešeren and Čop. The sadness that informs the poem may be in part due to Prešeren's realization that his access to fresh insights from European letters was to be severely curtailed as a result of his friend's death. The "exercise" was to lead him not to higher forms of poetic expression, but back to a simpler. less sophisticated kind of poetry. Poetically, the "Baptism" marked the end of the poet's most productive era.

For the non-Slovene the "Baptism on the Savica" must, like much of the rest of Prešeren's poetry, remain inaccessible.[131] Its very complexity, with multiple layers of meaning and involved poetic language, hinders its translation or, even when translated, its appreciation outside its native context. But like all the works of Prešeren's anthology and the miscellany not included therein, the "Baptism" deserves a closer look by the scholarly world and the general reading public. Despite all its complexity and the obscurity of the nation and language in which it arose, it still forms part, a very honorable part, of the European romantic epic tradition. It is the work of a genius of international significance who is still too little appreciated beyond the borders of his small homeland.

CHAPTER 6

German Poems

WITH the "Baptism" Prešeren's Slovene anthology closes. Though it contained most of his major works (and in our treatment here, has been supplemented to include all of them), one significant kind of poetry was absent from that slender volume's pages: Prešeren's works in German. As a complement to our very long chapter on his poetry, we deal with the best of those now.

Prešeren's German poetry is of two sorts, translations from his own Slovene texts (nine poems) and from Polish sources (four), and original verse compositions (twenty-one).[1] In a sense, all but the four Polish translations are Prešeren's original poems, for he alone composed them. His translations from the Slovene do display a bit more freedom in altering the original than a translator might otherwise permit himself. But on the whole these German translations of Slovene poems have no artistic existence independent of their function as translations. They were intended, as Robert Auty puts it, to serve as "propaganda" for the new Slovene literary language, so that those who read only German or read it more easily than Slovene might have some notion of what was happening in Slovene literature.[2] Since they were meant to be read together with their Slovene originals, the nine translations Prešeren did of his own poetry have been noted at the relevant points in the Slovene section of this book.

The remaining twenty-five texts include, besides the four Polish translations, two cycles of sonnets; a collection of satirical shorter pieces; seven individual sonnets; two elegies; and three miscellaneous pieces. It is apparent from the available manuscript evidence[3] that Prešeren had intended to publish some of these original works (ten, to be exact) with six of his own translations and one of the translations from the Polish as a later supplement to his *Poems* of 1846. Why he did not we can only guess, but his hesitance may have had something to do with the poor sales of the *Poems*. The German supplement never saw the light of day.

In our treatment here we have arranged the poems by genre, keeping to the spirit of Prešeren's arrangement of his Slovene poems. Within each genre the works are discussed in the order of their composition.

I *"The Literary Jokes"*

Prešeren was quite at home in German. Bilingual from childhood—his mother and uncles knew the language, and he was schooled almost exclusively in it from 1810 on[4]—Prešeren's poetic genius extended to both languages equally. Indeed, we sometimes get the impression from his German and Slovene poems that his talent exceeded the resources either language could offer him. His poetic diction is usually so flawless and unforced that the poet always seems in absolute and total command of his verbal instrument. Sometimes it even appears as if his poetic genius were independent of the languages he used, so easily did he move in and between them. No doubt this impression is erroneous. It certainly does an injustice to the effort the poet expended in composing his verse (effort we cannot know, for we lack his drafts). But Prešeren's great facility in German as well as his native tongue certainly allows us to conclude that the poetic gift had been given to him in double measure.

The poet's earliest original German poetry was a group of five satirical works entitled "Literärische Scherze in August Wilhelm von Schlegels Manier" [Literary Jokes in August Wilhelm von Schlegel's Manner, 1833]. Published in response to Kopitar's attack on the poet and Čop during the Ljubljana ABC War, they consist of a Latin epigram ("Error typi" [A Typographical Error]), in which Prešeren called Kopitar a small-minded critic, the Slovene sonnet "Apelles and the Cobbler,"[5] two German sonnets ("Relata refero" [I Repeat What I Have Heard] and "Hoc scio pro certo, quoties cum stercore certo" [I Know for Sure When I Fight with Manure]), and a German quatrain ("Du staunst, mein Freund" [You are amazed, my friend]). In the first sonnet Prešeren in no uncertain terms called Kopitar a plagiarist; in the second he characterized him as "piggish"; and in the final piece he ridiculed his "flailing" arguments. Even though in retrospect we may find Prešeren's treatment of Kopitar heavy-handed, yet we should keep in mind that these pieces are very much in response to some of Kopitar's own jabs, particularly his claim that Prešeren was vulgar. Moreover, from a literary point of view, though the purpose of Prešeren's satire has long since passed, we may still appreciate the poet's mordant wit. These "jokes" are among the funniest pieces Prešeren composed. Perhaps it is worthwhile mentioning here why he wrote them in German. According to Avgust Žigon,[6] at that time (the 1830s) only one person in the upper echelons of the provincial government could speak Slovene. Prešeren wrote his "jokes" in German, therefore, to be sure the local bureaucrats understood the issues between him and Kopitar.

II   "The Poet's Plaint"

A more serious cycle, yet not without a bite still, was to appear in the *Illyrian List* in 1833. Of the three sonnets submitted, however, only two were accepted. The third was turned down, no doubt for its personal attack on Kopitar. All three bore the superscription "Sängers Klage" [The Poet's Plaint, 1833]. The two that were published were also selected for inclusion in Prešeren's planned German anthology. Perhaps as a mark of his high regard for them, he planned to place them first and last there. We, too, must concur with the poet's judgment about these sonnets. As Auty puts it: "Formally these poems are most successful and show a complete mastery of the sonnet form. The language displays a rather classical idiom which was perhaps somewhat dated by the 1830s. Yet the combination of deeply felt emotion with strict form and dignified, allusive language results in poetry of unusual quality."[7]

The opening sonnet for the planned anthology, "Poet's Plaint I," would have been "Obschon die Lieder aus dem Vaterlande" [Although his songs had exiled him from the fatherland]. Preceded, as it was to have been, by the anthology's epigraph from Ovid, "I have written a small book in Getic [Gothic]," the poem continues the reference to the Roman poet who, having been exiled to the Black Sea, began to compose poetry in the local language. Ovid could not do without song nor suffer his sadness in silence. So he took to writing in a tongue he had not heard as a child. Like him, the Slovene poet has been severely criticized for his poetry. Therefore, to record his own grief, he has turned to a language he did not learn from his mother.

One can scarcely imagine a more powerful elaboration of Prešeren's plight than the one given here. In 1833 he had come under the heaviest attack to date from his Slovene detractors, so that he must indeed have felt like an internal exile in his own country. Cut off by "ill will" and "blind hate" from those he would normally sing to, he turns with shame ("Forgive me," he asks) to another language and audience to express his grief. In so doing, of course, he delivers his enemies a powerful reproach, for he clearly demonstrates how capable a poet he is in this alien language too. Thus even as a German-language poet his overriding concern is for the development of his mother tongue, for the implication of this first poem is that what he composes in German here he should naturally be composing in Slovene. Though a powerful expression, Prešeren's German poems are, he makes clear from the outset, a defeat for him and his greater interest, Slovene.

What was to be the closing sonnet of the German anthology, "Poet's Plaint II," begins "Wohl ihm, dem fremd geblieben das Erkennen" [Happy is he to whom awareness has remained alien]. The awareness in question is the biblical kind, which brought death in the end to humanity. Only one who is blind to that primal knowledge can be happy in this life, says the poet. He alone believes along with the fools that one should use the talents one has been given. He alone still believes in the ultimate victory of good. Unlike the poet, the blind man never doubts the outcome. The poet, on the other hand, full of the knowledge that "distorts, dissimulates, and demeans," must endure a life he finds absurd.

This treatment of the poet's deep-seated misgivings about life demonstrates his unerring ability to give personal expression to his ideas in German, too. For, regardless of the language, the point of view offered here is distinctly Prešernian; it parallels exactly what he said in so many of his Slovene works. The language has become merely a compliant creature in his hands for the expression of sentiments uniquely his own. To readers of his day, some of whom were, like the poet, equally at home in Slovene and German, this realization, when it came, must have been a surprise. In their midst was a poet who was capable of the most profound expression in German, a language in which they were accustomed to reading such poetic feats. But he was also capable of them in Slovene, where nothing of the sort had ever been done before. Even in "Poet's Plaint II," therefore, where the issue of language, Slovene versus German, is not addressed directly, it is handled implicitly. Every demonstration of the poet's prowess in either language, which led his fellow countrymen to an appreciation of him as a poet regardless of the language of composition, invariably led also to the elevation of Prešeren's Slovene to the level of honor held by German. His talent in two tongues served to equate them, an accomplishment never achieved before.

In the third sonnet of the cycle, "Ihr hörtet von der Zwerge argem Sinnen" [You have heard tell of the dwarfs' malicious designs], the poet descends from his lofty philosophical and linguistic considerations to a personal attack on Kopitar, whom he compares to a red-headed, greedy dwarf that is overly fond of young girls. While dwarfs, he says, are definitely creatures of the past, we have come across a modern equivalent: the dwarf? Kopitar. The young girl? Carniolan literature. The bolt he uses to keep her imprisoned? Censorship.

Certainly this is another of the sonnets Prešeren wrote in German in order to keep the Carniolan provincial government apprised of the events of the Alphabet War. It was, however, not published in his lifetime (it appeared in 1868), nor did the poet plan to include it in his German anthology. As a third "Poet's Plaint," it makes perhaps more of a point than one of the literary anecdotes with which he had criticized Kopitar earlier. For Kopitar is seen here not merely as the personal opponent of the poet, but as the violator of an entire literature through his abuse of his role as censor. The third sonnet, though very different in tone from the other two, rounds out the poet's lament by adding censorship to alienation and cynicism as enemies of a poet's happiness and sources of his plaint.

III   *Individual Sonnets*

There are seven sonnets in German which belong to no cycle. Several are occasional pieces, written to honor or commemorate some friend of the poet's, but the earliest had a very specific poetic purpose. "Warum sie, wert, dass Sänger aller Zungen" [Why is she, who is worthy that poets of all tongues, 1834] was published just shortly after the "Wreath." Why, the poet asks, is this girl, who is as worthy of praise as any other woman celebrated by poets from Homer on, praised only in Slovene, and not also in German? The answer Prešeren gives amounts to one of his most incisive social criticisms, as well as to a statement of love:

> Deutsch sprechen in der Regel hier zu Lande
> Die Herrinnen und Herren, die befehlen,
> Slowenisch die, so von dem Dienerstande;

Den strengsten Dienst dien' ich, den freie Seelen
Gedient, die Liebe schlug in ihre Bande,
Nicht darf ich gegen diese Sitte fehlen.

German as a rule is spoken in our land
By lords and ladies who command,
Slovene by all their servants.

The strictest service do I serve that free souls
Serve whom love wraps in its bands,
I must not violate this custom.

In all ways he is the underdog, helpless, as it were, to overturn the monopoly of German or the tyranny of his mistress. And yet the poem has a quite positive, almost defiant ring to it. The reason is, quite simply, that he has already challenged the hegemony of German, for he has sung the praises of his beloved in a form that no German poet has ever managed to use, the "Wreath." As yet unaware of the impossibility of his love for Julija, the poet in this sonnet still displays a confidence that his poetry can effect a change of heart on her part. Unfortunately, the poet's self-assurance was soon to be shattered forever by Julija's final rejection of him.

Of enduring worth, both as poetry and a statement of principle, is the sonnet, "Ihr, die entsprossen aus dem Slawenstamme" [You who have sprung from the Slavic stem, 1838], which was to have been the second poem in the proposed German anthology. The poet addresses himself to Slavs who write, like himself, in German. He does not condemn them, but he is angered when they prefer their "stepmother" to their "true mother," their Slavic tongues. This injustice must be corrected, he affirms. Yet, even at that, the "stepson" should be properly thankful to the parent who has adopted him by presenting her with gifts worthy of herself. She, who is "over rich," looks with scorn at trinkets.

Were there any doubts, this poem would resolve them, for it makes obvious that Prešeren considered himself above all a Slovene poet, yet one who would and could write well in German. As almost everywhere else in his corpus, he maintains an absolutely objective appreciation of the part German played in the culture of his country. He accepts good works of any kind and warns only against dilettantism, not linguistic exclusivism. In his own day this sonnet may have seemed a reasonable analysis of the local lingistic situation. From the perspective of our own time, however, its lack of linguistic nationalism may be somewhat surprising. As we have seen time and again in Prešeren's poetry, he was more interested in providing his language with poems than insisting abstractly on its prerogatives. Neither dogmatism nor purism had any place in his views on the proper development of Slovene. History has shown him to be correct: hence he, and not Kopitar, who was dogmatic, is the father of modern Slovene literature.

Another of the sonnets to have been included in the German anthology is "Nichts trägt an ihm des Dichtergeists Gepräge" [Nothing in him reveals the stamp of the poetic spirit, 1838]. It is couched in terms of Prešeren's poetic "swan song." How can he who so little resembles a poet write poetry, he asks. If he is in such deep despair, how can he make his love verses tolerable for those who do not share his misery? He is like the swan, he answers, who is dumb until he receives the death wound, then he begins to sing. He has been striken by the arrow: poetry has become his means of expression, and he can never recover.

In this sonnet, too, one of Prešeren's last, he still equates the erotic and the poetic impulses. Love alone, he claims, has been his stimulus, and especially the unrequited love which has made him so miserable. In many other romantic poets this stance would be in all probability a pose. The poet would assume it to heighten the respect he commands from his reader and to deepen the emotional charge of his verse. Prešeren, on the other hand, seems to have been completely sincere. He was genuinely in the impasse his poetry describes. When it came to depicting that crisis which so over-whelmed him at this time, he was capable, as this sonnet shows, of articulating his pain in German as well as Slovene. Both languages furnished a vehicle for his frustration.

IV *Elegies*

The central work of the German anthology was to be Prešeren's German-language elegy to Čop, "Dem Andenken des Matthias Čop" [In Memory of Matthias Čop, 1835], which was written and published less than three weeks after Čop drowned (6 July 1835). Composed in iambic pentameters with a terza rima rhyme scheme, the poem reviews Čop's life from the point of view of his friend who cannot cease lamenting him. The epigraph, given in Greek, is translated in the first line: "He dies young whom the gods love." The poet tells of the dreadful moment when he learned of his friend's death and saw his lifeless body. He depicts in intensely

bright tones where Čop died ("evening sun, green valley, giant
mountains in the distance, white clouds"), and why ("The world
spirit despatched his spirit from the hall of light, / To call you back
to light's companions"). Čop left the world at the peak of his
powers; he no longer has to bear the misfortunes of life—lovelessness, injustice, absurdity.

> Nicht mehr wird Dich die alte Wunde brennen,
> Dass fremd das Vaterland ist seinen Söhnen,
> Dass sie sich scheu'n Slowenen sich zu nennen,
> Dass abhold sie den teuren, süssen Tonen,
> In denen sie die Mutter auferzogen,
> Nur fremder Sitte, fremder Sprache frohnen.

> No more will that old wound burn you,
> That the fatherland is alien to its sons,
> That they are ashamed to call themselves Slovenes,
> That they are indifferent to the dear sweet sounds
> In which their mother raised them.
> That they chase after alien ways, an alien tongue.

Had Čop only lived, laments the poet, his erudition would have
made people proud of their country. Prešeren lists his friend's
languages and contributions: "Now death has taken you away from
us, / We saw the seed form so gloriously, / The true harvest day, it
will never come!" Finally he consigns his friend to eternal peace,
and promises, until he himself is carried to the grave, to lament the
untimely loss of Čop.

Much has been made of the philosophy purportedly underlying
the elegy to Čop, particularly Prešeren's use of the phrases "Welt-
geist" ("world soul") and "Urlicht" ("primal light"), which were
concepts prevalent in German thinking especially in the eighteenth
and early nineteenth centuries.[8] It is difficult to know, however,
whether the pantheism these words suggest is a genuine feature of
Prešeren's world view, or if, like the Greek paganism of the opening
and the muted Christianity of the closing (where the poet promises
his friend "endless peace" in death), they were not simply endemic
to the genre. What is clear from the elegy, however, is that death
came as a great release for Čop. It was the sure answer to all his
unhappy problems. Death, which occurs in the midst of the lushest
landscape Prešeren ever described, liberates, elevates, and purifies
Čop. Death's "sting" is not felt by its victim, but only by those who

must bear the loss of one they loved and needed. Even as he rejected suicide to solve his own problems, Prešeren remained, it would seem, attached to this vision of a liberating, kindly death. Death's refusal to come and liberate him without his taking his own life became one more of the frustrations that constituted for him the absurdity of life.

The other two elegies are little more than inscriptions for the headstones of Prešeren's friends. For Emil Korytko he wrote a simple quatrain which proposes that though the man die, what he has done for humanity lives on.[9] For one Maria Simonetti and her infant son he composed a sextain which consoles those left behind that we will all arise united from the grave "to go to our Father's eternal home."[10] These sentiments, both so appropriate to their genre, show Prešeren more as a versifier, that is, one who rhymes others' ideas easily, than as a poet with a single, coherent philosophy. The fact was that he could be both, depending on the circumstances.

CHAPTER 7

Conclusion

ACCORDING to Anton Slodnjak, Prešeren's greatest contribution to his nation was to have incorporated into Slovene literature "the most profound motifs of world literature" in a natural, compelling way, and to have made Slovene literature, thanks to the quality of the resulting poetry, worthy of the world's attention.[1] As we look back upon the poet from our late twentieth-century perspective, we see clearly that he was indeed the intermediary between European romantic culture and his fellow countrymen. He translated—in the root meaning of that word—into Slovene the most sophisticated products of the human mind and made them accessible to Slovene speakers in a way they never had been before. In effect he grafted a Slovene branch onto the European tree, so that the branch could grow more vigorously and the tree become more luxuriant.

Furthermore, in the 130 years since his death, Prešeren has become the embodiment of Slovene culture to the outside world. His poetry has come to stand as the highest achievement in the Slovene tongue. Wherever anything is known about the Slavic literatures of Eastern Europe, Prešeren is invariably included in the pantheon as the Slovene equivalent of the Russian Pushkin, the Pole Mickiewicz, or the Czech Mácha. We might recall here what Stritar said about Prešeren as the exemplar of the nation: that when they are called to give an account of their use of the talents bestowed on them by the Creator, the Slovenes will have to show but one thin book, Prešeren's *Poems*, to prove they have been faithful stewards of His bounty.[2]

While the national and international accomplishments of Prešeren deserve our close attention, I would submit here in conclusion that they still do not exhaust what we might say about the poet's greatness. Though we see him with the benefit of hindsight, we do not always perceive him correctly. For we tend to see the poet through his poetry. We frequently forget that his poems refract, they do not reflect, the circumstances of his life and the ideas he cherished. In a purely biographical approach to his work, where we assume that he speaks of himself in his poems, we receive a magnified and glorified picture of the poet's life. The facts cannot, however, be denied: Prešeren led an insipid, indeed on occasion a sordid life, relegated to an unrewarding job in a backwater of the Austrian empire, itself even in its most lively cities scarcely a center of the highest culture or scientific inquiry. The poet was a peasant's son with thoroughly bourgeois aspirations, relatively little drive, somewhat questionable sexual tastes, and an overaffection for the bottle. All this is not to condemn him; rather it is to point out Prešeren's greatest achievement. Despite the circumstances of his own life and the backwardness of his nation, somehow the poet transcended all his limitations, to compose poetry which examines the ultimate human problems and finds reasons for cherishing them all, even as they remain unresolved and tormenting.

The poet transcended his limitations and endured what, for his refined poetic sensibilities, must have been a hellish disparity between real life and the life of his mind. More than once he entertained thoughts of suicide, but he managed to overcome them. In fact, it was only when he stopped writing poetry that he successfully raised his hand against himself, to be saved at the last minute by some good but meddling soul. Perhaps, therefore, only his transcendent poetic state, even though it caused him great pain, gave him the strength to bear life. In the harmonies of his poetry, he found peace and logic, justice and freedom, the very rationale which alone enabled his sensitive, creative spirit to endure.

How can poetry with such an intensely personal purpose have a meaning for us, who are, Slovene and non-Slovene alike, now so different from Prešeren in time, temperament, and circumstances? The answer is that his poetry has more than one purpose, and even if we remain unmoved by the personal plight the poems depict, we still can benefit from the poet's transcendence in other areas. The poet sang to please his listeners with the sweetness of his language, the delicacy of his forms; to quicken their blood with erotic and patriotic visions; to ennoble his people through art; to enhance all human life by showing how its pain may be endured. Prešeren's poems are, in the parlance of the structuralists, saturated, polysemic. The only limitations on their riches are those imposed by the readers themselves. I hope this book has served to remove some of those limitations which time, language, or nationality have placed in the way of our enjoyment of Slovenia's premier poet.

Notes and References

Chapter One

1. Ivan Grafenauer, *Kratka zgodovina starejšega slovenskega slovstva* (Celje: Mohorjeva družba, 1973), pp. 21-23; also John A. Arnez, *Slovenia in European Affairs* (New York: League of CSAS, 1958), 29-39.
2. Grafenauer, pp. 38-41.
3. A word on language is appropriate here. Slovene is a separate and distinct Slavic language, with recognizable linguistic differentiation occurring as early as the tenth century (as evidenced by the so-called Freisingen Monuments, the earliest Slavic texts). Though similar to Kajkavian (one of the three major dialects of Serbo-Croatian) on the one hand, and some Slovak dialects on the other, these languages are not mutually intelligible without prior study. It was the belief of the early Slovene philologists, especially Jernej Kopitar, that Slovene was the oldest written Slavic language, because certain words in the modern language retain a shape very similar to words of Old Church Slavonic; considerations of relative age no longer carry any importance today, however. What does distinguish Slovene is its dialectal richness: given its size, it has an enormous range of dialects, more than any other Slavic language (cf. Tine Logar, *Slovenska narečja* [Ljubljana: Mladinska knjiga, 1975], p. 5).

Chapter Two

1. Grafenauer, pp. 105-7.
2. France Kidrič, *Prešeren 1800-1838: Življenje pesnika in pesmi* (Ljubljana, 1938), p. 8; hereafter *Prešeren*.
3. As Ivan Prijatelj points out (Ivan Prijatelj, "Duševni profili slovenskih preporoditeljev," in *Izbrani eseji in razprave* [Ljubljana, 1952], pp. 136-37; hereafter "Profili"), Jansenists, a conservative group of Roman Catholic clergy known for their severe morality, evangelical fervor, and basic humorlessness, in the latter part of the eighteenth century were instrumental in spreading literacy and piety to the masses of Slovene peasants. Only later did they acquire a reputation for narrow-minded intolerance of secular

143

things. The term "Jansenist" should properly be used in quotes for it was
shunned by the adherents of the movement itself (due to the Holy See's
disapproval of the philosophy), while being used largely by their detractors.
    4. For a discussion of this book in English, see Michael B. Petrovich,
"The Rise of Modern Slovenian Historiography," *Journal of Central
European Affairs* 22 (1963): 440-67.
    5. I do not wish to neglect a Slovene writer who was both a dramatist
and poet before Linhart and Vodnik, that is, Feliks Dev (1732-1786). His
melodrama *Belin* (1780) and his collection of his own verse and that of
others in "Writings" (*Pisanice*, 1779-1781), the first Slovene literary almanac, merit historical attention, but not literary.
    6. Josip Vidmar, "Dr. Francè Prešeren, 1800-1849," in *Poezije doktorja
Franceta Prešerna*, ed. Mirko Rupel and Alfonz Gspan (Ljubljana: DZS,
1949), p. 21; hereafter "Prešeren".

Chapter Three

    1. Fran Levstik, *Zbrano delo* (Ljubljana: DZS, 1948), 1:59.
    2. Grafenauer, pp. 152-53.
    3. Anton Slodnjak, *Geschichte der slowenischen Literatur* (Berlin,
1958), p. 121; hereafter *Geschichte*.
    4. Kidrič, *Prešeren;* Anton Slodnjak, *Prešernovo življenje* (Ljubljana,
1968); hereafter *P.ž.*; Boris Paternu, *France Prešeren in njegovo pesniško
delo*, 2 vols. (Ljubljana, 1976-1977); hereafter *Prešeren;* Avgust Žigon,
Prešernova čitanka: V dveh knjigah (Prevalje, 1922); hereafter *Čitanka*, are
the fundamental works, particularly Kidrič. They are the principal sources
from which I have drawn this and the following chapter.
    5. Paternu, *Prešeren*, 1:34.
    6. France Kidrič, *Prešernov album* (Ljubljana, 1949), p. 21, contains a
copy of his baptismal certificate.
    7. Kidrič, *Prešeren*, pp. 17-18.
    8. Ibid., p. 24.
    9. So his sister Lenka (born 1811) remembers in her memoirs (Tomo
Zupan, *Kako Lenka Prešernova svojega brata popisuje* [Celje: Družba sv.
Mohorja, 1933], as cited in Slodnjak, *P.ž.*, p. 8. This book, together with the
reminiscences of Prešeren's illegitimate daughter (Ernestina Jelovšek,
Spomini na Prešerna [Ljubljana: L. Schwentner, 1903]), are the two most
direct sources of information on Prešeren's personal life (his personal letters
are a third). Unfortunately, both are marred by the secondhand nature of
their subjects' knowledge: Lenka was born after Prešeren had gone off to
school, and Ernestina knew about her father only through the stories her
mother, Prešeren's common-law wife, chose to tell her. Kidrič uses both
these sources critically, and it is therefore upon him whom I rely for an
interpretation of them.
    10. Slodnjak, *P.ž.*, p. 10.

11. Kidrič, *Prešeren*, p. 26.

12. Slodnjak, *P.ž.*, p. 10; Henry R. Cooper, Jr., " Prešeren's Erotic Poetry," *Papers in Slovene Studies, 1978* (New York: Society for Slovene Studies, 1980), pp. 1-14.

13. France Kidrič, "Prešernove Lavre," *Ljubljanski zvon* 54 (1934): 549; hereafter "Lavre".

14. Ibid.

15. Kidrič, *Prešeren*, pp. 27-34.

16. Ibid., p. 96.

17. Ibid., p. 38; *Die Studentenweinvertilgungskommission*, as they called it in German.

18. Ibid ., pp. 129-30.

19. Ibid., p. 38.

20. Prijatelj, "Profili," p. 253.

21. France Kidrič, "Poslednja Prešernova Lavra," *Ljubljanski zvon* 55 (1935): 307; hereafter "Poslednja".

22. Kidrič, "Lavre," pp. 549-50.

23. Kidrič, *Prešeren*, p. 44.

24. Ibid.

25. Auersperg remembered his kindly master well, and after his death wrote a highly complimentary poem about him, "Remembrance of Prešeren" (*Nachruf an Preschern*).

26. Francè Prešeren, *Zbrano delo*, ed. Janko Kos, 2 vols. (Ljubljana, 1965-1966), 2:167-69; hereafter ZD. All references to Prešeren's writings are based on this two-volume collection of his complete works; all translations from his Slovene and German writings are by me unless otherwise indicated.

27. Kidrič, "Lavre," pp. 551-53.

28. Kidrič actually uses the term "first Laura" to describe a rather amusing "nonliaison" Prešeren may have had in Vienna. There he was charmed by the attentions paid to him by his landlady and her daughter— perhaps even to the point of writing for her some poems, although that is pure speculation—until he found out the daughter was already pregnant and quite desperate to marry anyone (ibid., p. 550).

29. *Povodni mož*, ZD, 1:72-75.

30. Its title was "Circumstances of Public Defense from all Areas of the Law and Political Science."

31. Kidrič, *Prešeren*, p. 60.

32. Slodnjak, *Geschichte*, pp. 111-12.

33. Letter to Čop, 13 February 1832, ZD, 2:174.

34. "Dekletam," ZD, 1:12; "An die Mädchen," ZD, 2:111.

35. Josip Stritar, *Zbrano delo*, ed. France Koblar (Ljubljana:DZS, 1955), 4:17.

36. Kidrič, *Prešeren*, p. 129.

37. Kidrič, "Lavre," pp. 612-14; Kidrič, *Prešeren*, p. 132; Slodnjak, *P.ž.*, p. 39.

38. Kidrič, "Lavre," p. 617.
39. Kidrič, *Prešeren*, p. 132.
40. Slodnjak, *P.ž.*, p. 42.
41. Kidrič, *Prešeren*, p. 147.
42. Ibid., pp. 121-23.
43. Prijatelj, "Profili," pp. 223-24; 224, n. 213; see also Gerald C. Stone, "Matija Čop's Correspondence with English Friends," *Papers in Slovene Studies, 1976* (New York: Society for Slovene Studies, 1977), pp. 24-55.
44. Ibid., p. 257.
45. "Slovo od mladosti," *ZD*, 1:109.
46. Slodnjak, *Geschichte*, p. 121.
47. Particularly "The New Way to Write" (*Nova pisarija*), *ZD*, 1:99-106; "Apelles and the Cobbler" (*Apel in čevljar*), *ZD*, 1:164; and "Hornets" (*Sršeni*), *ZD*, 1:113-17.
48. *ZD*, 2:112-14.
49. As cited in Žigon, *Čitanka* 2:39.
50. Cf. Sonnet 211 of Petrarch's *Triumphi*.
51. Though one shoulder, Ana Jelovšek made a point of remembering, was lower than the other, a fact Julija usually managed to conceal; as cited in Kidrič, "Lavre," p. 679.
52. Prijatelj, "Profili," p. 212.
53. Ibid., p. 263.
54. *ZD*, 1:107-8; 131-35; 165-70, respectively.
55. Kidrič, "Lavre," p. 683.
56. Paternu, *Prešeren*, 2:7-8.
57. Kidrič, *Prešeren*, pp. 264-65.
58. Ibid., p. 271.
59. Cf. ibid., p. 275, for details of Čop's death.
60. Slodnjak, *P.ž.*, p. 197.
61. Ibid., p. 288.
62. Ibid., pp. 290-92.
63. *ZD*, 2:95-98.
64. Ibid., 1:173-98.
65. Ibid., 1:172.
66. Ibid., 2:192.
67. Kidrič, "Poslednja," p. 310, where he says "Ana was a lover, not a Laura."
68. As a result of which he penned a sonnet (*ZD*, 2:115) which contains a severe criticism of Pavšek, another censor, and Stelzich, and names them in an acrostic.
69. Cf. Elinor Murray Despalatović, *Ljudevit Gaj and the Illyrian Movement* (New York: East European Quarterly, 1975), p. 201.
70. See below, pp. 54ff, for further information.
71. More of Prešeren's extant letters are addressed to Vraz (eight) than to anyone else, including Čop. They all, even when they contain disagree-

ments, are friendly; writing in German Prešeren regularly used the familiar "Du" with Vraz (*ZD*, 2:193-207).

72. Although on the matter of alphabet he did come around in the 1840s, when the "gajica," as it came to be called in honor of Gaj, gradually replaced the ancient but more cumbersome and less Illyrian "bohoričica." "Gajica" is the official alphabet in both Croatia and Slovenia today.

73. Kidrič, *Prešeren*, pp. 288-89; 336.

74. In a letter to Vraz, 19 July 1838, Prešeren complains of Gaj's calling him and Korytko "Carniolan separatists," and of his demand that "Carniolan tendencies" be removed from any folk songs they ask him to print (*ZD*, 2:199); cf. also Kidrič, *Prešeren*, p. 357.

75. Another attempt in the 1820s had failed. Cf. Anton Slodnjak, "Prispevki k poznavanju Prešerna in njegove dobe: I. Slavinja in Prešeren," *Slavistična revija* 2 (1949):1-29.

76. Slodnjak, *Geschichte*, p. 145, n. 1.

77. Smolè did manage, however, with Prešeren's help, to publish some of the Slovene literary "classics" he felt would be so important to a Slovene revival, as well as some of his own translations into Slovene of English plays.

78. *ZD*, 2:205, a letter of 29 July 1843; the deletion is in the *ZD* version. The name of Bleiweis's paper was *The Peasants' and Artisans' News* (*Kmetijske in rokodelske novice*); at first it was published in "bohoričica," but after 1845 appeared with more and more articles in "gajica," including some of Prešeren's poems.

79. Slodnjak, *P.ž.*, p. 241.

80. Kidrič, *Prešeren*, p. 275.

81. Kidrič, "Poslednja," p. 307. Kidrič is the chief source here.

82. Ibid., p. 306.

83. Kidrič, *Prešeren*, p. 218.

84. Cited above, p. 144, note 9.

85. Kidrič, "Poslednja," p. 315; she took up sewing.

86. Slodnjak, *P.ž.*, pp. 290-92.

87. Kidrič, "Poslednja," p. 307.

88. *ZD*, 1:40.

89. Slodnjak, *P.ž.*, p. 282.

90. Miklosich was to become one of the foremost Slovene scholars of the nineteenth century.

91. Slodnjak, *P.ž.*, p. 284.

92. Paternu, *Prešeren*, 2:258.

93. Ibid., p. 259.

94. Slodnjak, *P.ž.*, p. 286.

95. Paternu, *Prešeren*, 2:261.

96. Slodnjak, *P.ž.*, p. 290.

97. Kidrič, *Prešernov album*, p. 196.

98. By March 1849 only 318 copies of his *Poems* had been bought, for example (Paternu, *Prešeren*, 2:302; note the incorrect but frequently cited

148 FRANCÈ PREŠEREN

figure given by Žigon, *Čitanka*, 2:74, where he says only thirty-three were sold).

99. Cf. Stritar, pp. 9-10, where he writes: "Prešeren's life, what of it was shown to the world, was quiet, peaceful, quotidien, his entire existence was simple, customary, homey."

Chapter Four

1. *ZD*, 2:68: "Čudni dihur."
2. Ibid., 1:97-98: "V spomin Matija Čopa."
3. Cf. Janko Kos, *Prešeren in evropska romantika* (Ljubljana, 1970), p. 41, for a summary; for his viewpoint see pp. 53-54.
4. *ZD*, 1:97: "velikan učenosti."
5. Kidrič, *Prešeren*, pp. 120-21.
6. Cf. his correspondence with Fr. Savio: Fran X. Zimmerman, "Nova Čopova [Zhopova] pisma," *Veda* 4 (1914):97-118, 251-66, 380-92, with the supplement by Ivan Koštial, p. 392f., on previously published letters by Čop.
7. *ZD*, 2:68.
8. Kidrič, *Prešeren*, pp. 120-21.
9. Prijatelj, "Profili," pp. 221-24; 224, n. 213.
10. There are two editions of selected works by Čop, both with Slovene translations of his German writings: Matija Čop, *Izbano delo*, ed. Avgust Pirjevec (Celje: Družba sv. Mohorja, 1935), and Jernej Kopitar, Matija Čop, *Izbrano delo*, ed. Janko Kos (Ljubljana: Mladinska knjiga, 1973). Excerpts of his works in German can also be found in Jernej Kopitar, *Spisi*, ed. Rajko Nahtigal (Ljubljana, 1945), esp. vol. 2, bk. 2, pp. 339-52; bk. 2 covers the years 1825-1834.
11. These are gathered in "New Rejection of Useless Letters: That is: Slovene ABC War" (*Nuovo discacciamento di lettere inutili: Das ist: Slowenischer ABC-Krieg*), Supplement to the *Illyrian List* (Ljubljana, 1833), 17 pages. It includes: "Slovene ABC War" (Pt. 1, 30 March, 6 April, 13 April, 27 April, 1833 in the *Illyrian List*; Pt. 2, 6 June 1833; pt. 3, 27 July 1833, both in the *List*).
12. Cf. Kos, p. 44.
13. Slodnjak, *Geschichte*, p. 115; also Josip Puntar, "Dante in problem Prešernove 'nove pisarije,'" in *Dante*, ed. Alojzij Res, (Ljubljana, 1921), pp. 108-9.
14. Avgust Žigon, *Francè Prešeren: Poet in umetnik* (Celovec, 1914), p. 16.
15. Anton Slodnjak, *Pregled slovenskega slovstva* (Ljubljana: Akademska založba, 1934), p. 86; hereafter *Pregled*.
16. Paternu, *Prešeren*, 1:103-5.
17. Kos, pp. 45-46; based on Kidrič, *Prešeren*, pp. 225ff.

18. Cf. his article in the Kos edition of his selected works, pp. 174-79, where he speaks of Prešeren and the introduction of various new poetic forms into Slovene. See also Prešeren's letter to him (*ZD*, 2:177) where the poet asks his advice on a genre-related matter.

19. Prijatelj, "Profili," pp. 275-76.

20. Václav Burian, "Matija Čop kot Byronist," *Slovenski jezik* 3 (1940): 115.

21. Anton Slodnjak, "Slovensko romantično pesništvo in Schleglov Pogovor o poeziji" in *Študije in eseji*, ed. Jože Pogačnik (Maribor, 1966), pp. 88-91; *Geschichte*, pp. 114-21.

22. Čop (Kos edition), p. 170.

23. Cf., *ZD*, 2:86; "Ihr, die entsprossen aus dem Slawenstamme."

24. Cf. Slodnjak, *Geschichte*, p. 114; also Čop's letter to Kopitar, (Čop [Kos edition]), pp. 122-24.

25. Slodnjak, *Geschichte*, p. 114.

26. Kidrič and Slodnjak seem hesitant, for example, to acknowledge fully Prešeren's debt to Čop, as if it made the poet somehow a less brilliant or original thinker.

27. Slodnjak, *P.ž.*, p. 14.

28. Cf. Prešeren's epigram on his death: *ZD*, 1:116.

29. 13 February 1832 (*ZD*, 2:174); cf. also above, p. 26.

30. Ibid., p. 174, and to F. L. Čelakovský, ibid., p. 182.

31. Žigon, *Čitanka*, 2:28.

32. In the Klagenfurt journal *Carinthia*, 18 June and 24 September 1831.

33. Slodnjak, *Geschichte*, p. 131.

34. For a fuller discussion of Kopitar's ideas and their results elsewhere, see Rado L. Lencek, "Kopitar's Slavic Version of the Greek Dialects Theme," in *Zbirnyk na pošanu prof.-dr. Jurija Ševeľova—Symbolae in honorem Georgii Y. Shevelov* (Munich: Ukrainskyj viľnyj universytet, 1971), pp. 246ff.; hereafter "Kopitar".

35. Cf. "Patriotische Phantasien eines Slaven," in Bartholomäus Kopitar, *Kleinere Schriften*, ed. Franz Miklosich (Vienna: F. Beck, 1857), pp. 16-34; Prijatelj, "Profili," p. 181.

36. Prijatelj, "Profili," 178-79.

37. Cf., e.g., I. V. Jagič, ed., *Pis'ma Dobrovskogo i Kopitara v povremennom porjadke* (Saint Petersburg: Tipografija Im. Akademii nauk, 1885), p. 10, where in a letter to Dobrovský of 30 March 1808, he speaks of the purity of Carniolan Slovene because it lacks any but agricultural words; also Prijatelj, "Profili," p. 297.

38. Jagič, p. 92, letter to Dobrovský of 1/5 February 1810; he also extended this right to other Slavic languages, like Slovak; ibid., p. lxxxii.

39. Cf. Lencek, "Kopitar," for an exploration of this paradox, and also Rado L. Lencek, "The Theme of the Greek Koine in the Concept of a Slavic Common Language and Matija Majar's Model," in *American Contributions to the Sixth International Congress of Slavists, Prague 1968*

(The Hague: Mouton, 1968), pp. 199-225, for a "practical" elaboration of the "all-Slavic" literary language.

40. Slodnjak, *Geschichte*, pp. 111-12.

41. The year before the Styrian Slovene Peter Dajnko had published for Styrian writers his *Lehrbuch der windischen Sprache* [Slovene Primer], which was based on Styrian Slovene dialects and also advocated a modified alphabet, the "dajnčica"; it enjoyed a bit more success than the "metelčica," but was soon banned also.

42. *ZD*, 1:99ff.

43. Ibid., 1:165.

44. Ibid., 2:112ff.

45. In Kopitar, *Spisi*, pp. 321-39; the *List*, 6 July 1833.

46. Čop (Kos edition), p. 181.

47. Slodnjak, *P.ž.*, p. 140; Prijatelj, "Profili," p. 212.

48. Slodnjak, *Geschichte*, p. 113.

49. Ibid., p. 131.

50. Ibid., p. 129.

51. *ZD*, 2:192; 22 August 1836.

52. See "V spomin Matija Čopa," *ZD*, 1:97. "We are building ourselves a new bark, with a blessing we commit it to the waves, / It was not accustomed heretofore to avoiding the abysses, the rocks."

53. Hans Kohn, *Pan-Slavism: Its History and Ideology* (Notre Dame: University of Notre Dame Press, 1953), pp. 5-6.

54. Despalatović, p. 201.

55. Lencek, "Matija Majar," p. 205; "Kopitar," p. 249.

56. France Kidrič, "Osnove za Kollárjev vpliv pri Slovencih do 1852," in *Slovanská vzájemnost, 1836-1936*, ed. Jiří Horák, (Prague: Nakladem České akademie věd a umění a Slovanského ústavu, 1938), p. 131, also explores this paradox.

57. *ZD*, 2:181-83.

58. Ibid., pp. 184-88: letter of 29 April 1833.

59. Ibid., pp. 190-92: letter of 22 August 1836.

60. 10 March 1835, as cited in Žigon, *Čitanka*, 2:32.

61. Kidrič, *Prešeren*, p. 272.

62. Kos, *Prešeren in evropska romantika*, p. 216.

63. By Sir John Bowring in his *Cheskian Anthology* (London: Rowland Hunter, 1832), pp. 193-237; the collection is dedicated, by the way, to Čelakovský; Kos, *Prešeren in evropska romantika*, p. 214.

64. Bowring, p. 211 (stanza 45).

65. Kos, *Prešeren in evropska romantika*, p. 218; Kos calls the influence "more than likely."

66. *ZD*, 2:191; to Čelakovský, 22 August 1836.

67. Kidrič, "Kollárjev vpliv," pp. 131-32.

68. Despalatović, p. 90.

69. Ibid., pp. 129-34. Bulgarians, laboring under their own problems,

were completely untouched by the movement; the Serbs, initially hostile to Catholic Croatian suggestions in general, eventually joined with their Croatian Štokavian neighbors in signing the Language Agreement of 1850 in Vienna, which created a unified Serbo-Croatian, the principal positive result of Gaj's and Vuk's long efforts.

70. *ZD*, 2:199: letter of 19 July 1838 to Vraz.

71. *ZD*, 1:117.

72. Ivo Brnčič, "Ob veliki korespondenci," *Ljubljanski zvon* 66 (1936): 56-57.

73. That may be the import of Prešeren's statement of Vraz's difficulties with "The Baptism on the Savica," *ZD*, 2:193, letter of 4 March 1837 to Vraz; Prešeren and Kastelic could understand only half of the poetry written in Styrian Slovene, so he wrote, *ZD*, 2:195, letter to Vraz, May/June 1837.

74. *ZD*, 2:197.

75. Brnčič, p. 55; see also F. Petrè, *Poizkus ilirizma pri Slovencih* (Ljubljana: Slovenska matica, 1939), pp. 99-112, especially concerning Gaj's role in winning Vraz over to the Illyrian cause.

76. Žigon has outlined the Illyrian Movement in phases, *Čitanka*, 2:83ff.

77. Brnčič, p. 51.

78. *ZD*, 2:203: letter of 26 October 1840 to Vraz.

79. Ibid., pp. 193-94: letter of 4 March 1837 to Vraz.

80. Kidrič, *Prešeren*, pp. 288, 336.

81. Ibid., p. 350.

82. Slodnjak, *Geschichte*, p. 145, n. 1.

83. *ZD*, 2:198-200 and 201-3 respectively.

84. The Greek "το Παν" ("the all") is a pun on the Polish "Pan" ("Lord"); it strikes me unduly serious minded to read into this evidence of Prešeren's religious-philosophical beliefs, however.

85. Brnčič, p. 122: letters of Vraz of 1 August 1838 and 15 December 1840.

86. Slodnjak, *Geschichte*, p. 146; Paternu, *Prešeren*, 2:205.

87. France Kidrič, *Prešeren: I. Pesnitve, pisma*. (Ljubljana: Tiskovna zadruga, 1936), pp. 341-43: his letter of 7 September 1840.

88. Despalatović, p. 129; despite a similarity in names ("čbelica"— "bee"; "matica"—"queen bee") and function (nationalist publications), no direct connection seems to have existed between the Slovene and other South Slavic movements in the 1830s.

89. *ZD*, 2:205: letter of 29 July 1843.

90. For a good example, see Oton Župančič's speech to Maribor youth (Oton Župančič, *Dela*, ed. Cene Vipotnik [Ljubljana; Mladinska knjiga, 1967], 5:158), where a Christ-like Prešeren suffers for his people.

91. Prijatelj, "Profili," p. 309; cf. also I Prijatelj, *Slovenska kulturnopolitična in slovstvena zgodovina, 1848-1895*, vols. 1-5 (Ljubljana: DZS, 1955-1972).

92. Stritar, "Kritična pisma," vols. 5-6.

93. Ibid., p. 18.
94. Ibid., p. 28.
95. Ibid., p. 46.

Chapter Five

1. Slodnjak, *P.ž.*, p. 9.
2. Paternu, *Prešeren*, 1:45-47.
3. T. S. Eliot, *Selected Prose*, ed. Frank Kermode (New York: Harcourt, Brace, Jovanovich, 1975), p. 41 (from "Tradition and the Individual Talent").
4. Paternu's *Prešeren*.
5. Consider, for example, his explicit statement about genre-before-theme in his letter to Čop of 7 March 1832 (*ZD*, 2:177).
6. In this respect it is valuable to cite the interesting insight of Juraj Martinović, *Apsurd i harmonija: Jedno vidjenje Prešernovog pjesničkog djela* (Sarajevo, 1973), pp. 112-13, who claims Prešeren's "formalism" increased as the stresses in his personal life decreased his peace of mind. Thus too we might link his biography to his poetry.
7. In the interest of saving space, in this section I do not make specific reference to the individual poems. They are all to be found in *ZD*, vols. 1-2; the German version is entitled *Das freie Herz*. I must agree with Auty, "Prešeren's German Poems," *Oxford Slavonic Papers* 6 (1973): 5-7, that the German version is less successful than the Slovene original.
8. Paternu, *Prešeren*, 2:303-4, also insists on their variety and frequent "naiveness."
9. Slodnjak, *Študije in eseji*, pp. 114-20.
10. Paternu, *Prešeren*, 2:231.
11. A. V. Isačenko, *Slovenski verz* (Ljubljana, 1939), p. 20.
12. The German translation is *Macht der Erinnerung*.
13. The German translation is *Die verlor'ne Glaube*.
14. The German translation is *Der Seeman*.
15. Paternu, *Prešeren*, 2:247; this type of poem is well-known in English, too. Cf. George Herbert, "The Altar."
16. Edvard Kardelj (Sperans), *Razvoj slovenskega narodnega vprašanja* (Ljubljana: DZS, 1970), p. 282.
17. Slodnjak, *P.ž.*, pp. 255-56.
18. See Fr. Ilešič, *Prešeren in slovanstvo* (Ljubljana: L. Schwentner, 1900), p. 18, on the use of the terms "Slovene" and "Slovenia" in Prešeren's time.
19. W. K. Mathews and A. Slodnjak, *Poems by France Prešeren* (London: John Calder, 1969), p. 33.
20. Ibid., p. 34.
21. See studies by Čelakovský, Šafařík, Fr. Wollman, Kudělka, Isačenko, Burian, and others.

22. *ZD*, 2:206.
23. As cited by Paternu, *Prešeren*, 2:265.
24. Slodnjak, *Geschichte*, p. 144.
25. With the possible exception of the third, "Kdo učí," "who teaches," which, however, may be elided to an iamb.
26. Kos in his edition (*ZD*) has several more than ten. But since the remainder are sonnets, I have chosen to discuss them in the sonnet section of this book.
27. *ZD* 2:28, dated approximately 1845 by Paternu, *Prešeren*, 2:290.
28. Kidrič, *Prešeren*, p. 65.
29. *ZD*, 2:167-68: letter to his parents, 1824.
30. Especially David Strauss, *Das Leben Jesu*, which he liked so much that he lent it to people to read (Paternu, *Prešeren*, 2:132).
31. Kos, *Prešernov pesniški razvoj*, p. 224.
32. *ZD*, 2:79.
33. Kidrič, *Prešeren*, p. 160; Prijatelj, "Profili," p. 289, says he praised Christianity but did not include himself in it.
34. As outlined in Alex Preminger, ed., *Princeton Encyclopedia of Poetry and Poetics* (Princeton: Princeton University Press, 1965), pp. 712-13, "Romance."
35. Ibid., "Ballad," p. 62.
36. Only the patriotic theme is missing, if we accept Paternu's fourfold analysis of Prešeren's poetry into life and self, love, social-national-political (i.e., patriotic), and poetic (*Prešeren*, 1:107).
37. Slodnjak, *Študije in eseji*, p. 120.
38. Slodnjak, *P.ž.*, p. 180.
39. Each stanza is a quatrain, each line is composed of two hemistichs with a strong caesura. The rhythmic scheme is o ' o ' o ' o // o ' o ' o ', and the rhyme scheme is *a a b b*. See Preminger, p. 570, "Nibelungen Stanza."
40. Kos, *Prešernov pesniški razvoj*, p. 123.
41. Martinović, pp. 112-13.
42. Ivan Prijatelj, "Drama Prešernovega duševnega življenja," in *Izbrani eseji in razprave*, p. 357; hereafter "Drama".
43. So say Prijatelj, "Drama," pp. 355-57, and Kos, *Prešernov pesniški razvoj*, p. 128.
44. Mathews and Slodnjak, p. 78.
45. A certain parallel exists between Prešeren's attitude as expressed here and Dante's as we find it in his "New Life" (*Vita nuova*, translated with an essay by Mark Musa [Bloomington: Indiana University Press, 1973], p. 31 [sec. 18]).
46. Vidmar, p. 21.
47. *ZD*, 2:174: letter to Čop, 13 February 1832.
48. Ibid.
49. Ibid., 1:283-84.
50. Paternu, *Prešeren*, 2:281.

51. Others share the view that the poem is a failure, see Kos, *Prešernov pesniški razvoj*, p. 219.

52. That the "pisar" ("writer") is Metelko we have from a note written by Prešeren to Čelakovský; see Oton Berkopec, "Doneski k literarnim stikom Prešerna in Čopa s Fr. Čelakovskim in Fr. Palackim," *Slavistična revija* 13 (1961-1962):226. Also see Puntar, who views the poem as Prešeren's declaration of a Dantesque "dolce stil nuovo" for Slovene.

53. Cf. Francesco Petrarca, *Opere*, ed. Emilio Bigi (Milan: Mursia, 1963), p. 6.

54. Kos, *Prešernov pesniški razvoj*, p. 95.

55. Kidrič, *Prešeren*, p. 223.

56. Paternu, *Prešeren*, 1:130.

57. Stritar, p. 40.

58. Pavel Grošelj, "Prešeren in Petrarka," *Zbornik Slovenske matice* 4 (1902): 31ff.; Slodnjak, "Prispevki k poznavanju Prešerna in njegove dobe: III. Problem *Gazel*," *Slavistična revija* 4 (1951): 1lff. (Hereafter "III. Problem *Gazel*."); Kos, *Prešernov pesniški razvoj*, pp. 29, 132, 238.

59. Anton Slodnjak, "Prispevki k poznavanju Prešerna in njegove dobe: O Prešernovem *Slovesu od mladosti* in o literaturnozgodovinski rehabilitaciji Antona von Scheuchenstuela starejšega," *Slavistična revija* 9 (1956): 12 (hereafter "O Slovesu"), has a list.

60. Stritar, p. 17.

61. Slodnjak, "O Slovesu," p. 24; Ps. 90:10.

62. Slodnjak, "O Slovesu," p. 13; Rev. 6:12.

63. Slodnjak, *P.ž.*, p. 52.

64. Preminger, p. 323, "Glosa".

65. Valentin Vodnik, *Izbrano delo*, ed. Jože Koruza (Ljubljana: Mladinska Knjiga, 1970), pp. 36-37, "Moj spominik."

66. Paternu, *Prešeren*, 1:229.

67. Kos, *Prešernov pesniški razvoj*, p. 34.

68. Paternu, *Prešeren*, 1:177.

69. It is uncertain precisely when Prešeren wrote the ghasels. Here I accept the most recent hypothesis, which places the poems' origin at the end of 1832 (Slodnjak, "III: Problem *Gazel*," p. 17; Paternu, *Prešeren*, 1:296, n. 253).

70. See the epigraph to the first edition of the *Gazele* (*ZD*, 1:315) taken from folk poetry:

> Ljubézen je bila,
> Ljubézen še bó,
> Ko tebe in mene,
> Na svéti ne bó.

71. Preminger, p. 323, "Ghasel"; pp. 610-11, "Persian Poetry."

72. Who else but a friendly source would advise him to sing sonnets or ballads? Certainly not Kopitar.

73. Čop (Kos edition), pp. 173-75.

74. Sir John Bowring, pp. 193-237.

75. A fourth area of influence that was to gain some importance after the major sonnets of the poet had been written was the Polish, and especially the work of Mickiewicz. But Prešeren did not learn Polish until 1837, and then probably only poorly. Although he had been aware of Mickiewicz's and other Poles' writing from the mid-1820s, nonetheless it was only after 1837 that they had a direct impact on his poetry. But by then it was too late to influence the sonnets.

76. Paternu, *Prešeren*, 1:120.

77. Ibid.

78. But not the first sonnet. That distinction belongs to Jovan Vesel-Koseski, Prešeren's later nemesis, who in 1818 composed "Potažba" [Consolation], a mediocre effort at best.

79. Preminger, pp. 781-84, "Sonnet."

80. Slodnjak, "III: Problem *Gazel*," p. 12; Paternu, *Prešeren*, 1:124.

81. *ZD*, 1:298.

82. Slodnjak, "III: Problem *Gazel*," p. 21; also Paternu, *Prešeren*, 2:32, where there is a discussion of the possibilities.

83. Especially Petrarch's sonnets 3 and 211; Stritar, p. 40.

84. For that version, see *ZD*, 1: 324-30.

85. Preminger, p. 784, "Sonnet Cycle."

86. Slodnjak, "II: O Sonetnem vencu," pp. 241-42.

87. In most of the copies of *Poems* Prešeren changed several lines of the "Wreath" to undo the acrostic; only a few copies for himself preserve the name as in the original version of 1833.

88. Slodnjak, *P.ž.*, p. 143.

89. For a translation, see Matthews and Slodnjak, pp. 51-65; the English of sonnet 9 cited here is theirs. All other translations of the "Wreath" are mine.

90. Slodnjak, "III: Problem *Gazel*," p. 20.

91. Paternu, *Prešeren*, 1:246.

92. Ibid., p. 243.

93. Kos' division of the "Wreath" into units of 5-4-5 sonnets seems most correct to me, with the theme alternation going from erotic to patriotic to poetic, however; see Kos, *Prešernov pesniški razvoj*, p. 100.

94. Or as Juraj Martinović puts it, poetry was the one world in which Prešeren could create his own harmony (pp. 137-38).

95. Kos, *Prešernov pesniški razvoj*, p. 175.

96. Unless, of course, "Twice nine hundred and thirty-three," was written in 1838 or 1839; see above, p. 97.

97. *ZD*, 1:332.

98. All of the tercets of the post "Wreath" sonnets are rhymed in terza rima; cf. Zigon, "Tercinska arhitektonika v Prešernu," *Zbornik Slovenske matice v Ljubljani* 8 (1906):66.

99. Kidrič, *Prešeren*, p. 261.

100. A German translation also accompanies this poem, "Wohl gross war, Toggenburg, mein Schmerzgeselle"; *ZD*, 2:103. They were both published in 1836.

101. See also the sonnet in chapter 40 of Dante's *Vita nuova* (p. 83), to which it is obviously related.

102. With a German translation, "Aufthun wird sich, wenn das Gericht vollendet."

103. *ZD*, 1:339.

104. Lencek, "On Dilemmas and Problems," pp. 128-29.

105. Cf. Kopitar's *Grammatik der slavischen Sprache in Krain, Kärnten, und Steyermark* (Ljubljana, 1808), passim in introduction.

106. Cf. the note accompanying the 1833 publication of the poem, *ZD*, 1:341: "Um nicht mißverstanden zu werden, erklären wir, daß wir das Fach dem Hrn. K. als seine 'crepida' gelten lassen. Cuique suum. Wir beschränken daher diesen Anspruch lediglich auf sein *ästhetisches* Urtheil."

107. *ZD*, 2:251.

108. Martinović, p. 119, finds it too complex and bizarre for the cycle.

109. Anton Slodnjak, "Prispevki k poznavanju Prešerna in njegove dobe: IV. Sonetje nesreče," *Slavistična revija* 4 (1951):165; hereafter "IV: Sonetje nesreče."

110. Ibid., p. 173.

111. *ZD*, 2:190: letter of 22 August 1836 to Čelakovský.

112. Ibid.

113. Žigon, "Tercinska arhitektonika," p. 120.

114. For a brief summary of these views, see Slodnjak, *Geschichte*, p. 140; the latter comment belongs to Kos, *Prešernov pesniški razvoj*, p. 159.

115. See my article on Tasso and Prešeren ("Tasso and Prešeren's *Krst pri Savici*," *Papers in Slovene Studies, 1976*, ed. Rado L. Lencek (New York: Society for Slovene Studies, 1977), especially pp. 16-17, where I consider the problem of Prešeren's sources in the "Baptism."

116. *ZD*, 1:198, where the information appears as footnotes to the text.

117. Slodnjak, *P.ž.*, p. 192.

118. Cf., for example, Tone Šifrer, "Čop in Prešernov *Krst pri Savici*," *Ljubljanski zvon* 55 (1935):396; Paternu, *Prešeren*, 2:132-35; Kos, *Prešernov pesniški razvoj*, pp. 153-55.

119. I have numbered the stanzas here for convenience of reference; they were not numbered in the anthology edition of the poem.

120. See Slodnjak, *Študije in eseji*, p. 115, where he discusses the old man in each of those three poems ("*Prekop—Krst—Neiztrohnjeno srce*").

121. *ZD*, 2:190; also Slodnjak, ibid., pp. 122-23.

122. *ZD*, 2:177: letter of 7 March 1832.

123. Preminger, p. 595, "Ottava rima."

124. *ZD*, 1:356.

125. Paternu, *Prešeren*, 2:145.

126. Tercet 4; also stanza 39.
127. Stanzas 3-5.
128. Kos, *Prešernov pesniški razvoj*, pp. 152-55.
129. Slodnjak, *Študije in eseji*, pp. 114, 123.
130. Professor Slodnjak reports in his German-language history of Slovene literature (*Geschichte*, p. 153) that Prešeren may have written a novel in the 1830s, the manuscript of which might have made its way to North America. He asks there—and I gladly repeat his request—that if anyone is aware of the existence of such a manuscript, he or she would render Slovene literature an enormous service by making its location known.
131. Only the introduction has been translated into English, and that only in manuscript, by Anton Justin (item 1382 in Bulovec, cited immediately below). For a list of the translations into other languages, see Štefka Bulovec, *Prešernova bibliografija* (Maribor: Založba Obzorja, 1975), pp. 177-80.

Chapter Six

1. We must also add one Latin two-liner, "Error typi" [A Typographical Error], which is the first of his "Literary Jokes in August Wilhelm von Schlegel's Manner." R. Auty in his article on Prešeren's German poems attributes thirty-six German poems to Prešeren. The *ZD* contains only thirty-four, however, plus the one Latin epigram.
2. Auty, ibid., p. 5.
3. Cf. *ZD*, 2:286, for further information.
4. Kidrič, *Prešeren*, pp. 17, 19, 26.
5. Discussed above, p. 114.
6. Žigon, "Tercinska arhitektonika," p. 69, n. 1.
7. Auty, "Prešeren's German Poems," p. 9.
8. Cf. Paternu, *Prešeren*, 2:74-77, for a discussion of the various points.
9. *ZD*, 2:124: 1839.
10. *ZD*, 2:125: 1841.

Chapter Seven

1. Anton Slodnjak, "France Prešeren innerhalb der Weltliteratur," in *Aus der Geisteswelt der Slaven*, eds. Alois Schmaus and Ilse Kunert (Munich: Otto Sagner, 1967), pp. 115-16.
2. For a more recent and very convincing assessment of Prešeren's standing in contemporary Slovene literature, see Boris Paternu, "France Prešeren in naš čas", in *Sodobni slovenski esej*, ed. Janko Kos, (Ljubljana: Mladinska knjiga, 1979), pp. 337-45.

Selected Bibliography

PRIMARY SOURCES

1. Collected Editions

Francè Prešeren. *Zbrano delo*. Edited by Janko Kos. Vol. 1, *Poezije;* Vol. 2, *Nezbrane lirske pesmi. Nezbrane balade in romance. Nezbrani napisi. Drobiž. Nameček nemških in ponemčenih poezij. Nezbrane nemške pesmi. Prepesnitve ljudskih pesmi.* Zbrana dela slovenskih pesnikov in pisateljev, nos. 70 and 80. Ljubljana: Državna založba Slovenije, 1965 and 1966. The definitive modern edition of Prešeren's poetry and letters, with extensive notes by the editor; this is the edition used in this book.

Kerʃt per Ṣavici: Poveʃt v versih [*Krst pri Savici: Povest v verzih*]. Ljubljana: Joshef Blasnik, 1836. Prešeren's first separate publication, it is also available in a facsimile edition (Monumenta litterarum slovenicarum, no. 2. Ljubljana: Mladinska knjiga, 1967).

Krajnska zhbeliza [*Kranjska čbelica*]. Vols. 1-5 (1830-1848). Monumenta litterarum slovenicarum, no. 6. Ljubljana: Mladinska knjiga, 1969. A facsimile edition of the *Carniolan Bee*, which contains some of the earliest of Prešeren's poetry.

Pesmi Franceta Preširna. Edited by Jož. Jurčič and Jož. Stritar. Klasje z domačega polja, nos. 1-3. Ljubljana: Oto Wagner, 1866. The first critical edition of Prešeren's poetry to appear after his death. Especially Stritar's introduction to the volume began the "cult of Prešeren" as the greatest of Slovene poets.

Poezíje Dóktorja Francéta Prešérna. V Lublani: Natísnil Józef Bláznik, 1847. Prešeren's anthology, the only volume of his collected poetry to appear in his lifetime. It too is available in a facsimile edition (Monumenta litterarum slovenicarum, no. 1. Ljubljana: Mladinska knjiga, 1966).

Prešeren I: Pesnitve, Pisma. Edited by France Kidrič. Ljubljana: Tiskovna zadruga, 1936. The best of the pre-World War II editions of Prešeren's poems and letters, complemented by a second volume of Prešeren's biography. See Kidrič's *Prešeren 1800-1838*.

2. English Translations

LAVRIN, JANKO and ANTON SLODNJAK. *The Parnassus of a Small Nation.* 2d ed. Ljubljana: Državna založba Slovenije, 1965. Eighteen of Prešeren's poems are included in this English-language anthology of Slovene poetry, whose first edition was published by John Calder (London) in 1957 (it contained 16 of Prešeren's poems).

MATTHEWS, W. K. and ANTON SLODNJAK, eds. *Poems by Francè Prešeren.* 2d ed. London: John Calder, 1963. An enlargement of their *Selection of Poems by Francè Prešeren* (Oxford: Basil Blackwell, 1954), this book contains 46 English translations by several different translators and of varying quality. The entire "Wreath" has been included, as well as five of the seven "Sonnets of Unhappiness." No German poems were included. An introduction by Slodnjak gives a brief biography of Prešeren.

For translations of individual poems into English, as well as translations into other languages (German, French, Italian, Spanish, Hungarian, and the Slavic languages), see Bulovec's *Prešernova bibliografija,* pp. 127-287 (below).

SECONDARY SOURCES

AUTY, ROBERT. "Prešeren's German Poems." *Oxford Slavonic Papers* 6 (1973): 1-11. A useful analysis of Prešeren's German poetry, with a brief comparison between him and other bilingual poets.

BULOVEC, ŠTEFKA. *Prešernova bibliografija.* Maribor: Založba Obzorja, 1975. A complete bibliography of Prešeren's works, works about him, translations, and related matters.

BURIAN, VÁCLAV. "Matija Čop kot Byronist." *Slovenski jezik* 3 (1940): 106-24. An excellent article on Čop's role as the initiator of the cult of Byron among the South Slavs.

COOPER, HENRY R., JR. "Tasso and Prešeren's *Krst pri Savici,*" In *Papers in Slovene Studies, 1976,* edited by Rado L. Lencek, pp. 13-23. New York: Society for Slovene Studies, 1977. A study of the sources of "The Baptism on the Savica," especially Tasso's *Jerusalem Liberated.*

ISAČENKO, A. V. *Slovenski verz.* Ljubljana: Akademska založba, 1939. A study of Slovene verse, with much attention accorded to Prešeren and his verse forms.

KIDRIČ, FRANCE. *Prešeren 1800-1838: Življenje pesnika in pesmi.* Ljubljana: Tiskovna zadruga, 1938. The complement to Kidrič's edition of Prešeren; the most detailed account of Prešeren's life and the milieu in which he lived. Unfortunately never completed, the work stops ten years before the poet's death.

————. *Prešernov album*. Ljubljana: Državna založba Slovenije, 1949. Contains pictures and documents relating to all aspects of the poet's life.

————. "Prešernove Lavre," *Ljubljanski zvon* 54 (1934):547-53, 612-20, 675-86.

————. "Poslednja Prešernova Lavra." *Ljubljanski zvon* 55 (1935):305-16. This and the preceding deal with Prešeren's romantic attachments and their impact on his poetry.

KOS, JANKO. *Prešeren in evropska romantika*. Ljubljana: Državna založba Slovenije, 1970. A careful, detailed study of Prešeren's contact with the European romantic movement, and of foreign romantic influence on him. See also the lengthy review of the book by Boris Paternu in *Slavistična revija*, 19 (1971): 75-96.

————. *Prešernov pesniški razvoj: Interpretacija*. Ljubljana: Državna založba Slovenije, 1966. A study of the internal logic of Prešeren's poetic development.

KUDĚLKA, VIKTOR. "Kollárova koncepce slovanské vzájemnosti v jazykově literárním obrození Slovinců." In *Franku Wollmanovi k sedmdesátinám: Sborník prací*. Prague: Státní pedagogické nakladatelství, 1958. Pp. 115-28. A Czech study of Kollár's impact on the Slovenes, including Prešeren.

LAVRIN, JANKO. "Francè Prešeren, 1800-1849," *Slavonic and Eastern European Review* 33 (1954-1955):304-26. An English-language article on the life and work of the poet.

LENCEK, RADO L. "On Dilemmas and Compromises in the Evolution of Modern Slovene," In *Slavic Linguistics and Language Teaching*, edited by Thomas F. Magner, p. 112-52. Columbus, Ohio: Slavica Publishers, 1976. A thorough survey of the development of Slovene, including Prešeren's role in it.

MARTINOVIĆ, JURAJ. *Apsurd i harmonija: Jedno vidjenje Prešernovog pjesničkog djela*. Sarajevo: "Svjetlost," 1973. A Serbo-Croatian study of the poet's quest to find harmony in the midst of his life's seeming absurdity.

PATERNU, BORIS. *France Prešeren in njegovo pesniško delo*. 2 vols. Ljubljana: Mladinska knjiga, 1976-1977. The most complete modern treatment of all of Prešeren's poetry, seen within the context of his life. Very erudite, indispensable.

PRIJATELJ, IVAN. "Drama Prešernovega duševnega življenja." In *Izbrani eseji in razprave*, edited by Anton Slodnjak, 1:315-62. Ljubljana: Slovenska matica, 1952. His article of 1905 on the conflicts in Prešeren's spiritual life.

————. "Duševni profili slovenskih preporoditeljev." In *Izbrani eseji in razprave*, edited by Anton Slodnjak, 1:79-314. Ljubljana: Slovenska matica, 1952. His lengthy article of 1921, revised in 1935, tracing the history of the Slovene national awakening, treating among others Kopitar, Metelko, Čop, and Prešeren.

PUNTAR, JOSIP. "Dante in problem Prešernove 'nove pisarije.' " In *Dante*, edited by Alojzij Res, pp. 93-260. Ljubljana: Kleinmayr-Bamberg, 1921. A lengthy treatment of the impact of Dante's *dolce stil nuovo* on Prešeren's "new way to write."

SCHMAUS, ALOIS. "Prešeren's 'Taufe an der Savica.' " In *Studia slovenica monacensia in honorem Antoni Slodnjak septuagenarii*, edited by Hans-Joachim Kissling, p. 112-25. Munich: Trofenik, 1969. A study of the "Baptism" which in many ways summarizes Slodnjak's view of the epic.

SLODNJAK, ANTON. *Geschichte der slowenischen Literatur*. Berlin: Walter de Gruyter, 1958. An excellent German-language history of Slovene literature, with extensive treatment of Prešeren.

———. *Prešernovo življenje*. 3d ed. Ljubljana: Mladinska knjiga, 1968. One of the best biographies of Prešeren currently available.

———. "Slavinja in Prešeren," *Slavistična revija* 2 (1949):1-29.

———. "O Sonetnem vencu," *Slavistična revija* 2 (1949):231-49.

———. "Problem Gazel," *Slavistična revija* 4 (1951):10-22.

———. "Sonetje nesreče," *Slavistična revija* 4 (1951):162-76.

———. "Dvoje neznanih metrik iz dobe naše romantike." *Slavistična revija* 8 (1955):24-38. This and the preceding four essays form Slodnjak's series on Prešeren's poetry, with excellent analyses of the poems. Published under the collective title "Prispevki k poznavanju Prešerna in njegove dobe."

———. "Prekop—Krst pri Savici—Neiztrohnjeno srce." *Novi svet* 4 (1949):192-207. Particularly concerning suicide in Prešeren's life and work.

———. "O Prešernovem 'Slovesu od mladosti' in o literarnozgodovinski rehabilitaciji Antona von Scheuchenstuela starejšega." *Slavistična revija* 9 (1956):10-29. On the "Farewell to Youth."

———. "Slovensko romantično pesništvo in Schleglov Pogovor o poeziji." In *Študije in eseji*, edited by Jože Pogačnik, pp. 86-91. Maribor: Založba Obzorja, 1966. Additional articles outlining Slodnjak's penetrating views of various aspects of Prešeren's poetry.

ŽIGON, AVGUST. *Francè Prešeren: Poet in umetnik*. Celovec: Tiskovna Družbe sv. Mohorja, 1914. Still a controversial book containing theories about Čop and Prešeren that are currently not popular.

———. *Prešernova čitanka: V dveh knjigah*. Prevalje: Tiskovna Družbe sv. Mohorja, 1922. Contains useful original material (documents, a chronology) about Prešeren's life.

Index